PRAISE FOR
THE NEW SIRIAN REVELATIONS

"I've read all of Patricia Cori's books and loved every one of them—but this is the absolute best yet. I consider this to be one of the two most important books I have read in my life—the other being *The Tibetan Book of Living and Dying*. Filled with vision, and hope and truth, *The New Sirian Revelations* is a must read for every conscious being on the planet!"

—PETER BRIGHTMAN, CEO of International
Entertainment Corporation

"Twenty years ago a remarkable series of transmissions began from a six-dimensional collective, the Sirian High Council, to their scribe: Patricia Cori. This latest book is a most worthy successor to the original trilogy of Sirian Revelations and it is, quite simply, the best and most important book I have ever encountered. Each word radiates truth and illumines the path before us. If I could bring only one book with me to a desert island, it would be this."

—BRUCE STEFFEK, psychotherapist and coauthor of *Helping People Change*

"We must pay attention to Patricia Cori's messages from the Sirian High Council, our emergence into the galactic phase of coexistence is upon us and discernment in our communication, especially telepathically, is a priority. Listen closely and without reservation to their guidance about our ascension and heed their warnings—lest you get caught unaware and fall back into the matrix. Minus sugar coating, boldly unveiled in *The New Sirian Revelations* is our final step toward complete sovereignty . . . a must read!"

—DEBBIE WEST, journalist, host of Lost Knowledge Radio, and media spokesperson for the Extraterrestrial Civilization Scientific Research Network

"Patricia Cori has once again shown me the intense love the Sirian High Council holds for us—in very rich language, on a variety of subjects that describe, in a most intricate way, the beauty that awaits humanity. What they share in *The New Sirian Revelations* has touched me on the deepest level possible, broadening my perspective of our cosmic reality and accelerating my awakening."

—MAARTEN HORST, founder of ET-First Contact Radio

"*The New Sirian Revelations* is the ultimate quantum journey, a wake-up call for our times. From galaxies to gravity, wonder and pragmatism unite in this tour of the universe. This is a must-read for anyone willing to make a choice. Consumer or caretaker? Ultimately this book inspires hope: an empowering guide for a new heart-centered world. Patricia Cori excels as channel and scribe—bridging the Sirians' multi-dimensional perspective into a page-turning read."

—MAGS MACKEAN, author of *The Upside Down Mountain*

"A powerfully honest, yet loving, six-dimensional wake up call to all beings of our Sun System: human, earthly, and cosmic. During this paramount time in our collective unfolding and ascension, *The New Sirian Revelations* offers us awareness of the greater picture and a choice to play our important part in the symphony and Song of Creation. What a gift Patricia Cori has brought through for humanity!"

—KRISTIN HOFFMANN, composer, producer, and performing artist

The

NEW SIRIAN
REVELATIONS

ALSO BY PATRICIA CORI

The Cosmos of Soul: A Wake-Up Call for Humanity

Atlantis Rising: The Struggle of Darkness and Light

The Starseed Dialogues: Soul Searching the Universe

*No More Secrets, No More Lies: A Handbook to
Starseed Awakening*

*Where Pharaohs Dwell: One Mystic's Journey
Through the Gates of Immortality*

*Beyond the Matrix: Daring Conversations with
the Brilliant Minds of Our Times*

*Before We Leave You: Messages from the
Great Whales and the Dolphin Beings*

The Sirian Starseed Tarot

The Emissary: A Novel

The
NEW SIRIAN
REVELATIONS

Galactic Prophecies for the
Ascending Human Collective

PATRICIA CORI

North Atlantic Books
Berkeley, California

Published by
North Atlantic Books
Berkeley, California

Cover art © iStockphoto.com/RomoloTavani
Cover design by Jasmine Hromjak
Book design by Happenstance Type-O-Rama

Printed in the United States of America

The New Sirian Revelations: Galactic Prophecies for the Ascending Human Collective is sponsored and published by the Society for the Study of Native Arts and Sciences (dba North Atlantic Books), an educational nonprofit based in Berkeley, California, that collaborates with partners to develop cross-cultural perspectives, nurture holistic views of art, science, the humanities, and healing, and seed personal and global transformation by publishing work on the relationship of body, spirit, and nature.

North Atlantic Books' publications are available through most bookstores. For further information, visit our website at www.northatlanticbooks.com or call 800-733-3000.

Library of Congress Cataloging-in-Publication Data

Names: Cori, Patricia, author.
Title: The new Sirian revelations : galactic prophecies for the ascending
   human collective / Patricia Cori.
Description: Berkeley, CA : North Atlantic Books, 2017.
Identifiers: LCCN 2017038146 | ISBN 9781623171711 (trade paper)
Subjects: LCSH: Akashic records. | Parapsychology. | Prophecies (Occultism) |
   Human beings—Forecasting.
Classification: LCC BF1045.A44 C67 2017 | DDC 133.9—dc23
LC record available at https://lccn.loc.gov/2017038146

2 3 4 5 6 7 8 9 SHERIDAN 22 21 20 19 18

Printed on recycled paper

North Atlantic Books is committed to the protection of our environment.
We partner with FSC-certified printers using soy-based inks
and print on recycled paper whenever possible.

For my mother, Sara,
the brightest star of all.

CONTENTS

ACKNOWLEDGMENTS

For his receptivity to the idea of this new work, I would like to thank Tim McKee, the new publisher of North Atlantic Books, who set the pace for the book to be delivered at a time when so many readers have been asking for new Sirian Revelations. Janet Levin, senior director of sales and distribution, has always been my champion and a friend, and I am so grateful for and honored by that trust and support. To Adrienne Armstrong, the most amazing copy editor, who really gets the voice of the Sirians—a heartfelt thank you for your dedication—over the years, and several books later.

So many people contribute to the making of a book, it's difficult to name them all, so I reach out to all the people at North Atlantic Books who have helped bring this work to manifestation. Getting the cover image just right, and so vibrant a reflection of the content, is Jasmine Hromjak, art director; pulling all the details together and keeping me on track are editors Erin Wiegand and Ebonie Ledbetter. You are all so talented—thank you for bringing your gifts to the project.

And of course, there would be no project at all without the overlighting wisdom of the Sirian High Council, who have been with me for so long, helping me step forward on my life path and dedicating so much love and wisdom to the human race. How can words express the gratitude I hold in my heart for such a gift? Their presence has changed my life, and hopefully the lives of others, providing inspiration, wonder, and hope for our future, and for the way we choose to live our lives every day.

Finally, all of you, lightworkers, starseed, seekers—you are my family and I celebrate you and thank you, again, for your trust and all the love that pours from your hearts to mine, and back out, into the stars.

Last but never least, the wonderful friends who share my new life, encouraging me to make the moves and face the obstructions that have led me to my paradise world, where I live with rainbows and blue blue ocean—you know who you are. By my side are my kids, two gorgeous four-leggeds, Karma and Schooch, who waited patiently—curled up next to my chair in the wee hours of the morning, day after day, night after night—for their human to finish and go back to bed.

Every thought and intention that this book be born is woven into its pages. And I am grateful, and touched, by all of it and by everyone.

INTRODUCTION

1996—a mere twenty years ago. Some of you were not yet even a twinkle in your father's eye; many others of us were in various stages of crawling, climbing, and leaping through our own awakenings. Still others were completely asleep at the wheel, obliviously unaware of what was about to unfold, on the third globe out from our central sun—this place we lovingly call "Mother Earth," and even less conscious of what accelerating cosmic shifts were increasingly manifesting across our planet, in the plasma body of our sun, and throughout the entire solar system.

Bill Clinton, the forty-second president of the United States, was reelected to serve a second four-year term, as the leader of the so-called "free" world. Benjamin Netanyahu won Israel's elections the same year, becoming the country's youngest ever prime minister; Prince Charles and Princess Diana formally divorced.

The U.S. space shuttle Atlantis *docked with the Russian* Mir *space station, relieving Astronaut Shannon Lucid of her 181-day sojourn aboard the* Mir, *after setting a new American record for living off the planet.*

The total U.S. federal debt was $5.207 trillion. There were 5.76 billion humans inhabiting Planet Earth.

Iraq, Libya, and Syria were still sovereign nations, ruled by tyrants, no question—but still offering their citizens developed infrastructures, socially viable environments, and a civil framework within which to live.

Broadcast television giants, the primary networks, and technology industry leaders reached agreement on a new standard—high definition digital television—thanks also to Clinton's corporate-friendly deregulation of previous restrictions on the telecommunications industry. It was, to say the very least, broad-reaching in scope, set upon altering or, more succinctly, upon controlling every aspect of our lives, while providing unlimited corporate access to the unsuspecting minds of people worldwide—through programming, advertising, and electromagnetic entrainment.

This governmental overreach was to first lay the groundwork, and then to provide an unstoppable vehicle for some of the most insidious, dehumanizing systems that we have seen infiltrate every level of our global societies: unbridled consumerism, widespread pornography, trafficking of men, women, and children—and their organs, dependency upon technology, and the dumbing down of the population . . . because, as we all understand, an unconscious civilization is a controllable one.

I believe we will all agree that it has been a very effective "management tool" over the global population.

The World Wide Web was still in its infancy, at the onset of its future grip on global communications. A scant forty-five million people were using the internet then, thirty million of whom resided in North America.

While the assiduous telecommunications industry was accelerating its sweeping impact on and unrestricted control over the collective unconscious of the global citizenry, President Clinton chose August 7, the height of summer vacation season, to deliver news that should have bolted society from its deep slumber. Corroborating NASA's prior announcement, what he had to say, especially what he said between the lines, should have had the entire "tuned out" planetary population alert, and buzzing with excitement.

On that auspicious day, the president of the United States stood at a podium on the White House lawn and, reciting meticulously scripted words, quietly presented the world with a Martian meteorite, which, he asserted, showed possible evidence of an exoplanetary fossilized life form. In essence, he was telling us that NASA had unearthed an exciting new discovery that . . . well . . . might not be that exciting, since it was still inconclusive proof of the existence of ancient life on Mars. Nonetheless, it was going to be well worth going to Mars, with our six-wheeler par excellence, the Mars Pathfinder *rover, to find more rocks, to determine if life had ever existed in some remote, ancient Martian past.*

Never again, to my knowledge, did we hear of another potential biological fossil in any other Martian rock sample that the Mars Pathfinder *rover would have been able to collect and analyze for possible biological properties—which is, purportedly, why the multimillion-dollar rover was there to begin with.*

It didn't take a conspiracy theorist to glean, from the whole setup, that the real purpose of the rock, and the speech, was to inform us that it was the aerospace/military budget that was about to take a giant leap forward, into the great unknown, and that we, the taxpayers, were going to be funding it.

*As the official story goes, a curious team of snowmobile-riding geologists picked up a four billion year old rock, which just happened to be poking out from the snow-covered, icy tundra of Antarctica—waiting to be found. Ten years of elaborate study and laboratory analysis later (excuse me . . . that's **ten long years** later), they were finally able to identify it as a Martian meteorite.*

More . . . it seemed to contain a Martian fossil.

We were expected to believe that the absolute crème of the scientific world, with access to the most advanced technology, and working away in the secret laboratories of the U.S. government and its funded universities, spent the whole of ten years to determine that what they had plucked from the south pole was, in fact, a Martian meteorite. Really? It took ten years for the most highly paid teams of geologists, biologists, and NASA experts to analyze a rock containing a fossil? What looked to me, a layperson, like the undeniable presence of a fossilized life form, they told us, could very possibly represent "biological activity" of the ancient kind from that planet . . . but not necessarily.

Now that's what I call some pretty lame science.

Because the six brief paragraphs of President Clinton's message to civilization were only intended to receive a limited amount of media attention, at a time when hordes of Americans were at the beach, the Martian rock story came and went . . . relatively quickly. It barely made a dent in the wall of silence that held humanity back from accessing the wealth of information proving life beyond our planetary borders—and only delayed the inevitable: disclosure and contact.

Yet, it was so huge—something that would change every single human being's understanding of reality! On the one hand, those who believe that we human beings, along with the extraordinary display of biodiversity on this planet, are the sole life forms in this infinite universe might at least have questioned why the president of the United States was suggesting there could be reason to consider that, at the very least, little green bacteria might have existed in Mars's ancient past.

That should have blown the lid off skepticism.

On the other, those of us of the UFO/ET/conspiracy-theory persuasions, who have long understood that we are part of a thriving, bustling universe of living, conscious beings (some of whom are already present and walking among us), should have been asking ourselves: was this the springboard of the disclosure agenda, and was Bill Clinton positioned to be the disclosure president? But, as is the case with our highly distracted society, too few people were paying enough attention, or even feeling committed enough to insist that this existential question be addressed and answered—by the government of the United States, or by any other authority willing to lift the veil of secrecy that still shrouds the ET reality.

*The truth was that no authority **was** willing.*

Why was Clinton's strategic Martian rock pronouncement so underpublicized in the media? If the government (which we surely agree has denied us what they know of extraterrestrial life) was now showing us its willingness to at least consider it, then we were witnessing a big shift in position. Even if it was only a dribble—"possible" fossilized bacteria—surely this pronouncement should have made front-page news! The only plausible explanation that I can come up with, for that lack of media attention, is that the announcement was never meant to be more than a teaser to test public reaction.

Apparently, those in the power positions, who have dictated the course of civilization, thought that we, the "masses," were barely mature enough to contemplate the mere possibility of alien life—life that might have existed billions of years prior—much less to be faced with the truth about how it actually abounds across the universe. They weren't about to let us in on the fact that their secret government was already actively collaborating with extraterrestrials: in the space race to future galactic wars, the invasion of nearby planets, and their imminent enactment of absolute domination over our planet and our lives.

At the same time that they were monitoring our receptivity to the idea of life elsewhere, beyond Planet Earth, they were taking media manipulation over human perception to a new level of mass mind control, which, they were determined, would facilitate the implementation of the New World Order.

Until reaching the point where their social-engineering experiment would be too far-reaching for us to say "no," they did not want us to know about the advanced alien technologies that they would be utilizing, first to test and later to implement, as control systems over every aspect of our sovereign lives: within our bodies, upon the animals, lining our city streets, and monitoring us, from Earth's outer atmosphere. They certainly did not want us to know about races of alien origin: some entrenched in the underground; others, walking among us, right out in the open—so similar to human form they go relatively unnoticed, but for their haunting eyes and unrecognizable energy fields that the psychic eye cannot miss.

Most are complicit with our governments, trading futuristic, technological information for their freedom to experiment on humans and other life forms. They are intent upon the creation of a new hybrid species, merging human DNA with their own, or even worse—the assimilation of human DNA into complex computer biosoftware in cyborg robots—driving us quite rapidly into an insane reality, where biology serves and is completely controlled by artificial intelligence—and whereby we are enslaved, in every way possible, to technology.

Face it—we're heading there, aren't we?

Orwell, move over.

I think that we can agree and be clear about one very important point: the people at the very top, the puppeteers, have always been determined to hide from us their nefarious, covert interactions with certain alien species who are collusive with the secret government and, in significant ways, already directing the progression of earth affairs. They, the Dark Ops string holders, have always possessed the records of extraterrestrial intervention with humans, from as far back as the Sumerian record—those same records, left for humankind in a collection of imprinted clay tablets, that were either destroyed in the Iraq wars, or simply hidden away in their private libraries and vaults.

Sure, we were free to contemplate extraterrestrials all we wanted, provided we remained ignorant of the covert government/ET alliance, and so long as we remained in the dark as to where they intended to propel civilization through that exchange. If we continued to be terrified by media concoctions of monsters and demons from beyond, we were absolutely welcome to their depictions of archetypal alien villains, "invaders" from outer space, and their robotic intentions to destroy civilization and scorch the Earth.

We have had such extraterrestrial stereotypes designed for us for decades, and yet, hardly ever have we been allowed to consider the alternative . . . that there must surely be peaceful, loving beings from beyond, as well. Very rarely have we been invited to contemplate advanced civilizations, or been witness, through film and other media conceptualizations, to advanced worlds that—unlike ours—have overcome war, destruction, and the devastation of their own planetary resources.

It cannot be that the entire universe is composed of warring civilizations—such as ours! When we do catch glimpses of a peaceful exchange with beings from beyond, as in the case of the series Star Trek, *the "good guys" perpetually and inevitably face annihilation from the "bad guys"— depicted as hostile, villainous beings, across the universe. Almost always, the cowboys (the innocent) are the good, and the Indians (evil incarnate) are the bad. Yet, history has shown us, time and time again, that the opposite holds true. Still, that stereotype of good and evil is the formula that has served to perpetrate war, from time immemorial. It is no wonder that it is from this mold that humankind's fear of extraterrestrials has been cast, and it has held, for far too long, in our collective consciousness.*

As for the innocent little Martian rock discovery . . . consider, too, that, back in 1996, the U.S. government was still concerned about justifying the expense required to propel the space program into the twenty-first century—but not too concerned, of course, to land the first robot rover on Mars . . . just a year later, specifically, on July 6, 1997.

Ten years it took to find the rock, and to figure out that it was a Martian meteorite that appeared to contain organic fossilized matter . . . but only one insignificant year more, from that point, to position the rover on the Martian surface.

INTRODUCTION

What is wrong with that picture?
In that brief speech of August 7, 1996, Clinton told the world:

Good afternoon. I'm glad to be joined by my science and technology adviser, Dr. Jack Gibbons, to make a few comments about today's announcement by NASA.

This is the product of years of exploration and months of intensive study by some of the world's most distinguished scientists. Like all discoveries, this one will and should continue to be reviewed, examined and scrutinized. It must be confirmed by other scientists. But clearly, the fact that something of this magnitude is being explored is another vindication of America's space program and our continuing support for it, even in these tough financial times. I am determined that the American space program will put its full intellectual power and technological prowess behind the search for further evidence of life on Mars.

First, I have asked Administrator Goldin to ensure that this finding is subject to a methodical process of further peer review and validation. Second, I have asked the Vice President to convene at the White House before the end of the year a bipartisan space summit on the future of America's space program. A significant purpose of this summit will be to discuss how America should pursue answers to the scientific questions raised by this finding. Third, we are committed to the aggressive plan we have put in place for robotic exploration of Mars. America's next unmanned mission to Mars is scheduled to lift off from the Kennedy Space Center in November. It will be followed by a second mission in December. I should tell you that the first mission is scheduled to land on Mars on July the 4th, 1997—Independence Day.

It is well worth contemplating how we reached this moment of discovery. More than 4 billion years ago, this piece of rock was formed as a part of the original crust of Mars. After billions of years it broke from the surface and began a 16 million year journey through space that would end here on Earth. It arrived in a meteor shower 13,000 years ago. And in 1984 an American scientist on an annual U.S. government mission to search for meteors on Antarctica picked it up and took it to be studied. Appropriately, it was the first rock to be picked up that year—rock number 84001.

Today, rock 84001 speaks to us across all those billions of years and millions of miles. It speaks of the possibility of life. If this discovery is confirmed, it will surely be one of the most stunning insights into our universe that science has ever uncovered. Its implications are as far-reaching and awe-inspiring as can be imagined. Even as it promises answers to some of our oldest questions, it poses still others even more fundamental.

We will continue to listen closely to what it has to say as we continue the search for answers and for knowledge that is as old as humanity itself but essential to our people's future.[1]

While we were paying very little attention to what the presentation of rock number 84001 actually meant to the future of a covert space program pretending to be transparent, a certain Dr. Ian Wilmut, and his team of genetic adventurers, cloned a sheep named "Dolly" from adult ovine cells. It was "birthed," again to our relative lack of attention, around that exact same time—July of that year.

I was appalled at the overall lack of concern over what cloning animals would mean to our future, and flabbergasted at the lack of interest that news of this development solicited from people around the world. Was anybody, anywhere, paying attention to anything the government was concocting, anymore? The ethical questions racing around in my head, and screaming for answers, didn't seem to ring even a silent alarm in the minds of my contemporaries—but for a very few people, who were tuned in, with ears, eyes, and minds wide open.

Where was bioengineering headed? Would there truly be no significant ethical debate . . . reflection . . . or restraint?

What monstrosities would follow Dolly?

Unlike today's emotion-based media hysteria, which daily stirs its witches' brew of hopelessness, violence, and despair, the news networks kept a pretty tight lid on the story. The fact that a clone had been birthed in a laboratory, and was growing into an exact reproduction of its mother, just didn't seem to interest mainstream news, nor did it appear to raise the

---

[1] www2.jpl.nasa.gov/snc/clinton.html

proverbial red flag, in what was rapidly becoming a diminishing ethics dialogue between people around the world—including scientists, government officials, physicians, and futurists.

And yet, I believe this was an enormous leap into the deepest, darkest ravines in a futuristic landscape that involved not only human beings, but also all biological life on this Earth. Whereas man was already expert at creating death everywhere around him, now—thanks to secret laboratories pushing genetics and the manipulation of DNA—he was capable of unabashedly playing God with life: without the love, without the divine wisdom of how the perfection of Creation lies in its interdependency, harmony, and balance . . . and, as it had become clearly evident—devoid of all ethical considerations.

What aberrant creatures would come of that? How much more suffering would enslaved and tortured laboratory animals (and, eventually, human beings) have to endure in the name of "science"? I shuddered to think of where we were being taken, knowing, at the core of my being, that the mad geneticists' experiments had already propelled us to a dark place, somewhere between a horror movie and a science-fiction abomination, and that whatever they were concocting there, in the underground of genetic experimentation, would change the course of human evolution, and the biology of all life on our planet, forever.

During this innovatory time frame, the year of 1996, one of the most extraordinary crop circles of all time, the Julia Set, came down in a farmer's crop field—just across the road from Stonehenge, in Wiltshire, England— and I was there.

It was there and then, in July of that auspicious year, that I lay down in a field of wheat, where, inexplicably, an enormous array of circles—151 of them, to be precise—had been laid into the crop, in broad daylight. It displayed the perfect form of sacred geometry, the Fibonacci sequence: a mathematical growth pattern found in so many living things on Earth. Whoever or whatever had managed this monumental feat exhibited a keen knowledge of mathematics, ratio and proportion, which, in the end, is the perfect vehicle for interspecies communication, through which intelligence can usurp any language barrier, and be recognized, without question.

No sooner had I entered the field, and felt myself being pulled into the vortex of the formation, than I started spinning out of consciousness, losing all sense of being in body, connected to the Earth. I was catapulted into an extraordinary out-of-body journey that sent me sailing through the Milky Way, and other galaxies unknown, which I can only describe as the greatest astral voyage of my life!

I believe that it was during this experience that I was "reconnected" and attuned to a group of interdimensional light beings—vibrating as six-dimensional consciousness—whom we have come to know, through the first Sirian Revelations transmissions, as "the Speakers of the Sirian High Council." That incredible alliance has provided those who are ready to contemplate how conscious beings exist in higher dimensions, and how they perceive reality beyond our three-dimensional plane, with a window on the future of humanity—and a glimpse of the evolution of life beyond.

Through so many transmissions, and several books later, they have brought us accurate prophecy, guidance, and hope, above all . . . hope . . . that we are truly moving through this seemingly endless acceleration of violence and confusion, on our way to something quite spectacular.

I speak for all of us who are centered in love, and seeking peace, when I say, "Come on, change! Let's get this party started at last!"

My direct channel to the Council is still open and pure. The night oil burns again, and what new insights and prophecy they have to share, at this pivotal moment for us all, are flowing through me, to form the written manuscript you are about to read: The New Sirian Revelations. Unfettered access to such extraordinary light beings still serves as my compass, my lighthouse through the roughest seas of my own emotions. It helps me navigate my way, and hopefully yours, through the mass of confusion and deliberate disinformation *being dished up to humankind, in these quite turbulent hours of unfathomable change on every level—where storms are unrelenting, everywhere around us.*

Throughout this remarkable personal mission as their scribe, I have been honored to share such profound insights with you, galactic visions that have been life-changing for me, at a very personal level, for I have learned, above all, to live in the present moment, and in wonder of the future . . . rather than in fear of the unknown. They have drawn us a schematic of the immeasurable: new understandings of an infinite multiverse that has no beginning, no end, and no limits whatsoever. They have shown us how we, the microcosmic representation of that infinite field of possibility, are just as boundless and immortal as the universe itself, for we are made of the same stuff: atoms, protons, electrons, and the design of Prime Intelligence, compassion, and love.

They have not shied away from showing us the very real issues that are driving our societies into total upheaval. They never have. The Council's earlier warnings have pretty much all come to pass, just as they foresaw them. These included pleas and specific messages regarding the health of our oceans, from the Great Whales and the Dolphin Beings: those who are still embodied here on Earth, as well as those who have already ascended and gone on to serve as galactic weavers of frequencies upon the cosmic seas.

Their prophetic messages have proven themselves, time and time again, to be accurate depictions of our present, a world that has been described in so many indigenous prophecies, particularly those of the Maya and the Hopi. Both perceived great cosmic cycles as the passage from one great galactic age to another. They both predicted Earth, and the cosmic influences involved with our solar system, to be at the point of an enormous shift, from 2012 onwards—the turning of a mighty wheel, which has been referred to as "the Great Shift of Ages."

Many people interpreted the fact that the Mayan calendar ran out in 2012 as a harbinger of disaster, but in reality, what these ancient star people were leaving for future civilizations was their legendary understanding of the nature of time.

The Mayan calendar depicted that time—recorded time—would disappear. Found chiseled into that great stone masterpiece were symbolic clues to untold mysteries regarding the course of humanity, and its place in the cosmic order, but none was more relevant to us today than the ending of their calendar. Rather than warning of the end of times—to some apocalyptic destruction of all life upon our planet—the calendar's finality speaks to the eventuality of our shifting out of the space-time continuum, and of our moving into a dimension where time would no longer be relevant.

The Sirian teachings, regarding our passage out of the space-time continuum, mirror much of Mayan wisdom. Or, perhaps it is the other way around, and it was the Mayan wisdom that mirrored Sirian perspectives, for the Maya were accessing all manner of galactic information from the Pleiadians and Sirians as well—and it is to the fifth and sixth dimensions where five million Maya ascended, before their civilization mysteriously disappeared.

The Sirians are dedicated to helping us experience the joy of this transition, one that they lived through hundreds of thousands of years ahead of us. It is not always easy information to absorb, for, in an effort to empower us, they have exposed so much about the dark forces determined to take Earth down to the lowest vibrations—and, let's face it: that is not information we want to hear.

However, they insist, and I wholeheartedly agree, that our willingness to understand the adversities facing us—never denying but, rather, understanding how and why we have come to be in the throes of such an ultimate struggle of darkness and light—is ultimately highly empowering.

Bold we must be to acknowledge that there is a spiritual war under way on this planet, for it helps us to understand far greater forces at work here, and, as determined lightworkers, it renders all the more spectacular our vision of what light can do. It illuminates our imagination, allowing us to visualize the most breathtaking new landscapes that will be ours to experience, upon this Earth in transition.

The Speakers remind us how, at this moment, we appear to be on our knees, crawling through a field of tangle weed, still blinded to the utterly glorious view of the blossom that is filling the fields of our Earth, with the scent, the color, and the texture of new life, awakening to its spring.

Like nurturing parents, they push us, gently, to rise and stand tall in the wake of change. Beauty abounds. There is the new, just up ahead, calling us forward. And nothing—no amount of darkness or ill intent—can stop humanity from rising, once again, as it did after the fall of Atlantis.

In the earlier works, and now, in this new volume of messages, the Council has provided detailed observations of what awaits us, as we accelerate and attune to higher frequencies, where—at long last—we will be free to experience ourselves from beyond the confines of the third dimension.

They have always spoken of our passing from this reality to the next, and of the ascension of our sun and all the planets of this solar system, but from our current vantage point, it is still so difficult for us to grasp what that truly means. What is a higher dimension—a place of being without form, without self-awareness? Is it a parallel universe, adhering to the same laws of physics, or does it exist outside those assumptions? Will we be ghost-like apparitions of our former physical selves?

How we long to know—to truly know—what lies ahead. We want to know viscerally, experientially, without doubt and beyond measure. And yet, it is the not knowing, the intangibility of that sense of future, that motivates us to always keep seeking . . . to keep reaching for the stars.

We are soon to discover what the sun's immortal journey holds in store for us—as individuals, as the collective human race—and even for our beautiful Earth, a celestial being of incredible power and beauty. She holds us in her grace, as she traverses the physical universe, and prepares to move beyond it.

What a process for me personally, and for all of us, being gifted with visions of a world struggling through its paces, ascending to a higher consciousness—a world that still must be cleansed, and purged of its darkness.

The Sirian High Council has repeatedly referred to this time of intense change as "the Desert Days." In their previous books of Sirian Revelations, they spoke of us being about to "walk through the Desert Days," after which we would find ourselves in the light of a more refined resonance frequency. They described a preliminary encounter with our collective and personal karma, which will stand before us, awaiting resolution. In turn, we will then be clear to proceed to a more loving, peaceful state of consciousness, one we so long to know after our exacerbated struggles here, in the drama of our present times, have pushed us to the brink of disaster—on moral, ethical, and physical grounds.

Many of us now understand, much more succinctly, that to which they were alluding. We, the awake and awakening stewards of this magnificent blue-green planet, recognize how we are dragging ourselves through allegorical barren lands to loftier plains. We are eager to heal ourselves, as we long to restore the vast oceans, blue skies, fertile soils, and the crystalline mantle of our jewel in the universe to their pristine forms.

What we have yet to imagine—what eludes us, as we do our best to cope with all the elements that define our present geopolitical, ethical, and ecological struggles—is how the higher realms ("dimensions," as we have come to understand them) will manifest for each of us . . . and for the collective. Can it be we are truly going to be capable of overcoming our seemingly insurmountable turmoil, to finally take our place in the Alliance for Intergalactic Commerce and Cultural Exchange?

Twenty years to the day of those first transmissions, the Sirian Emissaries are back, sharing new and prophetic visions for the ascending human race, as we proceed—stumbling at times, soaring at others—through the outer reaches of the fourth dimension, to new levels of conscious awareness and parallel realities . . . in preparation of our imminent emergence.

They have given us time to grow and to learn, and more importantly, they have awaited our first encounters with the clearing station of the fourth dimension, before returning—to help us understand what is happening, and how this all will manifest. So many of us know, through increasingly frequent and bizarre events—and our observations of ourselves moving through them—that we are already experiencing it.

Here, at the early stages of our bridging from the third dimension to four-dimensional reality, unthinkable scenarios are now playing out in our fields of consciousness—on both ends of the spectrum. At a time when some of us are experiencing incredible openings in our ultrasensory skills and capabilities, and while, constantly, the Earth is unveiling the unwritten truth about the true past of humanity, discord and violence appear to be completely out of control . . . and escalating to untenable extremes.

A sense of vulnerability and fear is touching our lives personally now, as human conflict is no longer somewhere far away, beyond the reach of our personal lives—a news story somewhere "over there." As growing disharmony expands around the planet, incited and perpetuated by those who want to keep us divided and drowning in the quicksands of our lowest emotions, we recognize how human beings seem to be glued to conflict: with each other, and against the very nature of Earth herself.

It seems there is almost nowhere left on our planet, where peace reigns sovereign, and where the land, sky, and waters are untainted and pure.

We are being forced to really examine and take to heart the human condition, with all its injustice, with so much unnecessary suffering, and with such ignorance of the world in which we live—a planet that was meant to be revered and nurtured, so that, in kind, it would provide for all of our needs. But conflict is an agenda, and we have yet to overthrow its orchestrators. Until we do, chaos—in all its manifestations—remains front and center, staring right into our faces, demanding resolution.

We can no longer remain anesthetized to the fact that, somewhere else, in a place we used to ignore by simply turning off our televisions, innocent men, women, children, and animals are suffering immensely from the inhumane conditions fraught of war, brutality, and poverty. We can no longer avoid feeling their anguish and terror, or facing the consequences of how that suffering spirals into the darkest emotions—ones that, in turn, are instrumentalized to stir further the discontent and disempowerment of the global society.

Their suffering is now our suffering. And that place is now our backyard.

It has come full circle, pushing its way into our consciousness. It is everywhere around us now, personal enough for us to feel its effect on our individual lives, our neighborhoods, and society at large. Even the elite, in their castles, and the wealthy, in their gated communities, are feeling the pressure slamming up against their protective walls, for nothing can hold back the tidal wave of rage and revolution.

In the heartfelt words of the great Reverend Martin Luther King Jr., sentiments that linger in our hearts and minds, we are reminded that "only love can do that."

The Sirians want to help us to understand that what we are actually facing through all of this upheaval is our collective karma, the countless millennia of discord on the planet and within the human spirit. We now have the opportunity to resolve it, so that we may step up to the frequencies of a solar system about to pass through its sun's vortex—its astral cord—to experience itself as a higher vibratory essence: to be lighter, brighter, and more centered in peace, unity, and love.

As we are facing that discord, so are we also blessed with the karmic consciousness of the highest intellect, consciousness, and awareness of illuminated individuals and civilizations from loftier times, when humanity reached for the stars!

Light and dark, love and fear—all of this is contained in our karmic satchel, which we, the human race, have carried into the twenty-first century, as we hike through the Desert Days . . . on our way to the clearing.

At the onset of this, their latest missive, the time is July 2016—a mere twenty years later, but, oh, how our lives have changed! A staggering 3.5 billion people, almost half of the entire global population, are now plugged in to the internet. The human race has exploded to 7.5 billion people—a thirty percent increase in only two decades—and we are expected to exceed 8 billion within the next few years.

Unless drastic changes are enacted, Earth will soon be unable to sustain the volume of consumption generated by so many human beings, still dramatically unaware of their abuse of the planet's resources.

From the first stages of cloning life, to the insanity of creating chimeras of human and animal DNA, mad scientists now openly admit to cooking up hybrid organisms in their genetics laboratories. We "conspiracy theorists" know they are decades ahead of what they're telling us. If they are finally going public with some of their biological experiments, we can pretty much *count on the fact that they have been at it for forty or more years, and that they are well beyond the preliminary experimental stages.*

We have gone from six carefully crafted paragraphs of information on the late-night news about a "rock from Mars," to mainstream media hype over a manned mission to that planet, and its colonization, possibly as soon as 2020—a mere four years forward from the time of this writing.

The projected U.S. federal debt for 2016 is estimated to reach a staggering $19.3 trillion by year's end. That is 350 percent of what the national debt was twenty years ago!

War, the most profitable business on the Earth, is expensive.

We are being groomed for the next phase of techno-biological existence as cyborg, exoplanetary emigrants off the Planet Earth, for reasons that should at the very least concern us, while the rulers of our world do everything they can to destroy the planet, as quickly and efficiently as possible.

Something is very wrong at the top, to say the least.

Fortunately, though, through the eyes of the Sirians, we are privy to a multidimensional perspective that still is difficult for us to imagine, bound, as we are, to the events of our rapidly changing world—but it is exciting, and filled with hope, empowered.

As we observe political corruption, absolute techno-insanity, and the total militarization of our world, the Sirians are helping us awaken to the fact that we are already into the Great Shift of Ages, and that the old is, indeed, giving way to the new. Like all cyclical manifestations of energy and life, death of the old, the shedding of the skin, opens the way for new life—the birthing of new form. And like a mother on the birthing chair, having to bear the unbearable, it hurts.

This is excruciating pain, and many of us do not acknowledge or remember signing up for it. What's more, we refuse to believe that, on some level, we have co-created it . . . just to be part of its resolution. That sort of cosmic responsibility eludes us, even in the best of times.

Now, as this beautiful planet shudders and shakes . . . as our global climate and natural resources are being manipulated and deliberately destroyed . . . as we bomb the soul out of the Middle East, and then wonder why world demographics are changing so dramatically—the new is being birthed.

The old is going: kicking and fighting all the way.

Right on schedule, ancient monarchies and their reigns, false prophets, corrupt leaders, and secret government cabals, with their clutch on the planetary soul, are being taken down, as prophecy from many different seers and ancient societies foretold. The systems that had been put in place to dominate the Earth and deny us our liberation from their controls—described and prophesied, with uncanny accuracy, in the trilogy of Sirian Revelations (The Cosmos of Soul; Atlantis Rising; No More Secrets, No More Lies)*—are coming apart at the seams. This has either already come to pass, or it is manifesting in the unfolding of current events.*

At a time when we suffer from the degradation of humanity all around us, the struggle between darkness and light being fought at every level, and untold blight being perpetrated upon the Earth, that is good to know. Let the old give way to the new, and let us stand, united, to reconstruct the sister/brotherhood of Earth, as we go careening into the future, on our way to extraordinary galactic and conscious discoveries!

Let us take enormous comfort in the fact that the Sirian High Council foresaw and told us how this time of immense upheaval would signal the last phase of our passage—out of the darkness, and into the light of far more illuminated states of being.

As you leaf through the following pages, let your heart, once again, serve as the screen for what touches you through these words, filtering and accepting only that which rings true to you—as it has in the past.

May we always remember, and be calmed in the knowing, that when we review those earlier works, we cannot help but admit . . . they have not been wrong yet.

And that can only mean that we are almost through the storm, on course, sailing toward the horizon.

1

The Earlier Transmissions

Prophecy Unfolds

Over the twenty years that I have been privileged to serve as scribe to the Sirian High Council, I have had to be bold, overriding my own limited perception of the nature of the universe: matter, energy, stars, planets, galaxies, and dimensions. I have had to neutralize any judgment I would feel during the process of serving as their channel, in order that, with as much purity and objectivity as humanly possible, I might bring through to you their visions of our personal and planetary future.

Their prophetic messages have probed the full spectrum of our experience, for the Council has always been determined that we understand the range of energies that seem to be colliding with each other, but that, actually, are a natural reflection of the three-dimensional world in which we live—an inherent state of imbalance, pushing us forward to seek and then find resolution.

To do that, we have been called upon to understand how opposition works—what fuels it, and how it resolves—because, in their wisdom, the Sirians have always reminded us that only by understanding conflict can we ever heal it. Being willing to explore all aspects of duality, we enable ourselves to fearlessly manage our own lives and our societies. We learn to see everything as energy and its physical manifestation, and, in so doing, we become far more empowered in our determination to deliver our world, and a more loving, peace-seeking human collective, to the next dimension.

To clearly convey the power of that intention has meant being meticulously careful not to water down the information, nor to censor it in any way, which was quite an undertaking, particularly considering the general lack of awareness, and available resources, back then—before our expanding global awakening took us to where we are now, twenty years later.

Their truth and oracular visions of what was to come on Earth, and throughout our solar system, did not conform to just about anything else we were hearing at the time of their emergence in my life—beginning in 1996, when I returned from my life-altering experience in the Julia Set crop circle in England, and initiated the process of channeling their messages.

Serving as a completely impartial transmitter of six-dimensional wisdom was, and continues to be, an enormous challenge, considering the implications of prophecies they stated with uncanny precision—at times, alarming; at others, breathtakingly filled with light—and what they meant to our expanding awareness of reality beyond our immediate planetary borders . . . even beyond our physical universe.

Any responsible channel knows she or he must deflect influences from other sources, whether conflicting or not, to keep the channel pure and untainted. In a time such as ours, with such a wealth of data, theory, and conjecture bombarding our every thought, that requires a considerable commitment, and focused intention. I take neither of these lightly, constantly calling myself to integrity and reliability for all concerned, and I take this opportunity—the onset of a new compendium of Sirian teachings—to thank you all for your trust, and for the confidence you have expressed, from the beginning, in the intention behind my commitment to bring these works to you.

Over the years, the Speakers have shown us an expansive landscape of this revolutionary time on Earth, and more than just a glimpse of a brilliant horizon—rising, over the mountaintop. We are eager witness to the spectrum of that light—from the inky darkness of deepest night, to the sweetest violet and magenta hues of dawn—and we are living each phase, every shade and color, trusting that fully luminous skies are our destiny.

Several human beings, those we refer to as the "sleeping," or the "dark-intended," choose to hold their gaze on the shadow, almost mesmerized by it—never looking up . . . never trusting the light. Others, conversely, refuse to see anything but that light, denying that there is also wisdom to be gleaned from stories that lie buried in those valleys and that soon—and this is the most important point of all—even the darkest ravines and gutters will be illuminated.

Only by acknowledging both, the darkness and the light, can we truly see the greater picture. The Sirians have always provided their visions of that full scope of experience and information, and I trust that The New Sirian Revelations *will live up to that promise: helping us to see the light ahead, yes, but also fearlessly looking into the darkness that we came to help lift into that light.*

Clearly, we were being given revolutionary information that would serve as tools to push us through those barriers placed upon our road to higher consciousness by whatever forces were determined to deter us from our spiritual destiny. The Council's observations and teachings provided us with handbooks to alternative health and social responsibility. These were specific guidelines for us, as individuals, that showed us how to surmount the obstructions, and to take our rightful place as true guardians of our world in transition—caretakers of the very soul of Gaia.

It would be up to us whether we would use them for the ultimate personal and societal good, with clarity of purpose and intention, or whether we would ignore what was unfolding around us—absorbed into the holographic matrix of twenty-first-century technology, as willing subjects for the experiment under way: turning human society into a computer-controlled, robotic wasteland.

My mind grappled with otherworldly, seeming impossible visions of their macrocosmic picture of Creation, and our role in all of it—souls in passing . . . starseed in transit—currently serving as guardians, on the third orb out from the sun. Was humanity truly ready for a giant leap? Could we really effect the changes necessary to bring our struggling planet, our global civilization, and ourselves to a higher harmonic resonance? And if we could—would we?

Extreme earth changes are manifest now, constantly, perpetually, everywhere on the planet. Some say the last two decades have been the most destructive of the world's ecosystems, and the most damaging to Earth's atmosphere, of any time in our planet's (estimated) five billion year history. With such limited historical records, we cannot know that for certain. But we do know that, while the never-ending sociopolitical battle thunders, as to whether or not there is truly a case for global warming, the poles are melting, weather is raging out of control, and we are witness to the mass extinction of animal and flora species, and the death of oceans, around the globe.

From my own very human perspective, and as a concerned resident of our struggling, perpetually assailed planet, I confess that, as I was hearing this information, which then spoke of our imminent ascension to a less dense, less polarized dimension, I couldn't help but wonder if we would really make it. How, I asked myself, would we reach that state of consciousness that would propel us forward, when there was so much to heal and rebalance on our beautiful blue-green sphere in the heavens?

4

And then, of course, there was the question of the source itself, and how it would be perceived. Admittedly, I wasn't looking forward to being labeled, criticized, and critiqued for presenting myself as a "transmitter" for disembodied messengers from higher dimensions, and I did have moments when I considered aborting the mission altogether. Fortunately, I had the strength and conviction to override that concern and to do it anyway. That choice has made all the difference in my life and, I am honored to say, in the lives of so many like-minded souls.

I was fortunate to have the endorsement and support of committed, enlightened publishers: first, with Gateway Books in England, and then later, with my current publisher, North Atlantic Books, who have never faltered in their intention and express desire to bring the Sirian wisdom to you all.

To my amazement, and to that of so many readers over the last twenty years, those prophecies either have come to pass or, at the very least, have been validated by scientific and intellectual societies that previously relegated channeled material to the "tinfoil hat" category of New Age delusion. New science, particularly the evolving field of quantum physics, validates more pieces of their visionary puzzle every day, and so much of what the Sirians prophesied has already become manifest reality, in these volatile first years of our twenty-first century.

We have entered into a new galactic cycle. I doubt that anyone alive on the planet, and that includes the most remote tribes in what remains of the deep Amazon jungle, would disagree that there are huge shifts occurring in the skies, the waters, and the ground of Planet Earth.

In an extraordinary radio interview (later transcribed in the book Beyond the Matrix[2]*) that I conducted with the highly respected astrophysicist and co-founder of String Theory, Professor Michio Kaku, we spoke of how science was catching up with spirit—an incredible shift in the polar divide*

---

[2] Patricia Cori, *Beyond the Matrix: Daring Conversations with the Brilliant Minds of Our Times* (Berkeley, CA: North Atlantic Books, 2010).

between two planes of perception. How refreshing it was to engage in a dialogue with a man considered to be the "Einstein of our times," and to contemplate, together, how empirical knowledge and esoteric wisdom were uniting to form a new understanding of the meaning of life and Creation. That alone spoke to me of the emergence of a new level of consciousness!

Considering the accuracy of the Council's prophecies, which began two decades ago, I am filled with personal certainty that these, their new visions for the next phase of our development—solar ascension—will again guide us to a clearer understanding of the essential nature of our earthly process: an evolutionary destiny that promises the incredible—as it is seen through their loving eyes.

Let us take a look at some of the underlying themes and predictions that formed those threads of prophetic wisdom, from as far back as 1996, when their first messages wove themselves into the tapestry of Sirian Revelations.

They revealed orchestrations of a secret government, puppeteering world leaders under the management of an elite group of earth-based reptilian aliens, the Annunaki, for reasons that have to do with reducing Earth's vibratory frequencies, in order for our planet to reach resonance with theirs. I speak, of course, of Nebiru, the now infamous "Planet X," which is still careening through space—caught in an orbit between Sirius and our star, Ra. According to the Council, these beings believed that, by creating a resonant vibrational frequency with our Earth, their dying civilization, imprisoned inside that roving planet, could escape its dark destiny by managing to loop an electromagnetic lasso around our planet, hitching a ride to the fourth dimension, when Earth ascends from the constraints of the physical universe.

As "loopy" as that sounded at the time, this galactic scheme appears to reflect NASA's current thinking on celestial mechanics.

Today, on NASA's own website, one can read the following:

Caltech researchers have found evidence suggesting there may be a "Planet X" deep in the solar system. This hypothetical Neptune-sized planet orbits our sun in a highly elongated orbit far beyond Pluto. The object, which the researchers have nicknamed "Planet Nine," could have a mass about 10 times that of Earth and orbit about 20 times farther from the sun on average than Neptune. It may take between 10,000 and 20,000 Earth years to make one full orbit around the sun.

"The possibility of a new planet is certainly an exciting one for me as a planetary scientist and for all of us," said Jim Green, director of NASA's Planetary Science Division. "This is not, however, the detection or discovery of a new planet. It's too early to say with certainty there's a so-called Planet X. What we are seeing is an early prediction based on modeling from limited observations. It's the start of a process that could lead to an exciting result."[3]

It should be noted that this planet, and its rulers, are known in the ancient Sumerian texts, respectively, as "Nibiru" and the "Nephilim," as elaborated by noted scholar and academic Zecharia Sitchin. In his collection of scholarly books, The Earth Chronicles, *he interprets the ancient hieroglyphic record as rendering the Nephilim, or Annunaki, as bringers of light to the Earth, gods among men, who accelerated the development of our civilization.*

The Sirian High Council does not see them so favorably, presenting us a cautionary view of these beings. They describe them not as gods, but as an alien, reptilian civilization whose ruling class has interfered with our progression—from the stripping of our DNA light codes, to the massive disruption of our global ecology, our worldwide economy, and every aspect of our interactive global society.

Perhaps what is most fascinating about the existence of Nebiru, and its interference with the Earth, is presented in the second book of the Sirian Revelations: Atlantis Rising. *In it, the Council describes how Nebiru, orbiting Sirius C, was expelled during that star's ascension out of the third dimension. According to their description of celestial dynamics at work in that process, it careened back to Sirius A (that star we all know as the bright blue star on the horizon, the closest star to our sun), and then got caught*

---

[3] http://solarsystem.nasa.gov/planets/planetx

in a gravitational volleyball game, of sorts, between the two stars: Sirius A and our sun.

Contrary to the precept that all planets orbit a central star, this idea has been described in a 2011 report, published in the Monthly Notices of the Royal Astronomical Society, *in an article entitled "How Planets Can Survive a Supernova" by Andrew Fazekas.[4] In it, the author described this process, years later, as a scientific theory. Eerily mirroring information received from the Sirians in 1998, the article states, "When a star dies in a violent supernova, some of its planets may survive the blast but be ejected from orbit and sent wandering the galaxy."*

Amazingly enough, and echoing the Council's very precise information regarding how Nebiru, ejected from Sirius C's ascension process, became captured between Sirius A and our own star, Fazekas quotes the study leader, Dimitri Veras, an astronomer with the University of Cambridge, as saying:

> Because every star dies, and many of these stars are massive enough to trigger planetary ejection, there is ample opportunity throughout the galaxy for stellar deaths to contribute to the free-floating population. We don't know yet how common these planets are, but the observational evidence suggests that there could be more planets floating in between stars than orbiting them.

Giving credence to one of the most difficult concepts in the Sirians' explanation of Nebiru, and its underground surviving civilization, careening through space, the article also describes the possibilities of such ejected planets hosting—you guessed it—underground life. According to John Debes, a postdoctoral fellow at NASA, an ejected planet could possibly survive "if it had enough internal heat and already supported subsurface life."

---

[4] http://news.nationalgeographic.com/news/2011/08/110805-planets-survive-supernovas-ejected-rogues-space-science/

Once science achieves an understanding of how, rather than dying (described as "going supernova"), the very soul of the star is actually ascending, it will be replicating, with precision, the Sirian Revelations that were given to us twenty years ago, before quantum physics moved from the hallowed halls of academia, and began to take hold in our new awareness of the universe. Then again, we are still so far from reaching common ground regarding our own immortality, always questioning what happens to the human soul when it separates from its body, that it is understandable how difficult it is for us to even contemplate such processes at the cosmic level: the idea that the spirit of planets, of stars, perhaps even of whole galaxies, eventually ascend to higher dimensions, leaving their physical forms behind.

I confess to laughing out loud when I read that NASA was planning to "lasso" an asteroid, in order to drag it into a stable orbit around Earth's moon. Didn't the Sirians use the exact same terminology? It sounded so out-rageous, back when we published the book Atlantis Rising, *which described in detail how the Nebiruans were trying to lasso the Earth, in some electro-magnetic, interplanetary resonance field of their electronic design, so that our planet could drag theirs through the ascension cords of our sun.*

That was some pretty far-out, hypothetical physics, to say the least, that we were presented with back then, and I found it so unfathomable, on the one hand—and so totally logical, on the other. Yet, I was very conflicted about bringing it forward to my readers, knowing it could only challenge people's credulity. Imagine my amazement when I found it, years after, leaping off the pages of NASA's own press release!

Just a few years ago, we learned that NASA is planning a smaller ver-sion of that very idea, and they have mirrored the Council's own words to describe the invasive and mechanical manipulation of celestial bodies in space. On their own website,[5] the agency openly discusses their plan for asteroid repositioning, as follows:

> NASA has identified multiple candidate asteroids and continues the search for one that could be redirected to near the moon in the 2020s.

---

[5] www.nasa.gov/content/what-is-nasa-s-asteroid-redirect-mission

Since the announcement of the Asteroid Initiative in 2013, NASA's Near-Earth Object Observation Program has catalogued more than 1,000 new near-Earth asteroids discovered by various search teams. Of those identified so far, four could be good candidates for ARM. Scientists anticipate many more will be discovered over the next few years, and NASA will study their velocity, orbit, size and spin before deciding on the target asteroid for the ARM mission.

NASA plans to launch the ARM robotic spacecraft at the end of this decade. The spacecraft will capture a boulder off of a large asteroid using a robotic arm. After an asteroid mass is collected, the spacecraft will redirect it to a stable orbit around the moon called a "Distant Retrograde Orbit." Astronauts aboard NASA's Orion spacecraft, launched from a Space Launch System (SLS) rocket, will explore the asteroid in the mid-2020s.

The robotic mission also will demonstrate planetary defense techniques to deflect dangerous asteroids and protect Earth if needed in the future. NASA will choose an asteroid mass for capture with a size and mass that cannot harm the Earth, because it would burn up in the atmosphere. In addition to ensuring a stable orbit, redirecting the asteroid mass to a distant retrograde orbit around the moon also will ensure it will not hit Earth.

If NASA is indeed planning to lasso asteroids in a very few years, in order to pull them into orbit around the moon (the true reasons for which I doubt will be revealed to us before they actually manage it), surely the Sirian explanation of how the rulers of Nebiru intend to lasso the Earth, for purposes of their planetary survival, is no more far-reaching or phantasmagorical.

Apparently, if Dr. Kaku has it right, we metaphysicians may soon be able to exchange ideas and theory with the scientific world—without being cast as "tin hats" in the arena of cosmic debate. I have been told by the mother of a NASA employee that they possess an enormous library there, of every science-fiction novel ever written, and of all manner of alternative books and theories regarding just about everything. I was delighted to hear my books were there, too! I delight in contemplating how perhaps, just perhaps, the brainiacs of NASA may be getting at least a little inspiration from outside their vast sources of "scientifically sourced" data—from science-fiction writers, and from those of us who claim and believe we are channeling information from higher dimensions.

No matter how our diverse visions or beliefs present themselves, or how they are received, as a communal experience of what is truly going on out there, in the galaxy of worlds and beyond, I believe we can all agree—that here, on our tiny ball in space, dateline 2016/2017—one thing is certain: we are moving precipitously through the fantasy realms of science fiction, surpassing them, catapulted on a rocket of new thought, into an unprecedented new age of unfettered technology, futurism, and cutting-edge science.

The perception of black holes, as incredibly destructive vortices supposedly left by dying stars in supernova, seems to be rapidly evolving to something far more complex and exciting in the scientific community, thanks to visionaries such as Stephen Hawking. Although Einstein's Theory of Relativity (published in 1916) predicted their existence, he himself actually did not believe in them—or, shall we say, that his primary theorem did not allow for them to exist? And yet, he did believe in "bridges" in space-time, his term for our current, conceptual "wormhole," as a shortcut through space and time.

Later, in 1935, Albert Einstein and fellow physicist Nathan Rosen actually predicted that these bridges existed in space-time, based on Einstein's original theory. So, in other words, Einstein did not believe in the model of the black hole as a "collapsing of matter," caused by the gravitational force that would create the hole itself . . . but he did believe in wormholes, possible parallel universes, and tunnels in material space.

Astrophysicists, like Hawking, are finally putting together a new vision of Einstein's theory, one that reexamines black holes to actually be those wormholes, or portals, to other material worlds existing on the space-time continuum, or even further: passageways to other universes, even other dimensions.

The Sirians described in great detail how black holes were exactly that: celestial bodies' astral cords, leading the planet's own soul, or spiritual essence, to other universes and dimensions.

This assertion was absolutely contrary to the scientific information at that time, even Hawking's original observations, which determined black holes to be vortices of immense gravitational force that would crush and reduce, to the densest matter, anything that came into their field. This he described as "singularity."

In a recent article, entitled "Quantum Gravity Takes Singularity out of Black Holes," published in New Scientist *magazine,[6] author Katia Moskvitch describes new scientific theories regarding this very question. She states:*

Falling into a black hole may not be as final as it seems. Apply a quantum theory of gravity to these bizarre objects and the all-crushing singularity at their core disappears. In its place is something that looks a lot like an entry point to another universe. Most immediately, that could help resolve the nagging informational paradox that dogs black holes.

Hallelujah! Although conventional physics still insists on the singularity—the "crushing gravity" depiction—of black holes, master physicists are now reexamining their own earlier theories and observations. Their recent evolution seems to align with what we were told in the very first book, The Cosmos of Soul, *in which the Sirians described the nature of black holes, and their purpose—cords through which spirit passes from one dimension to another—in space.*

How absolutely stunning that quantum theory is now concerned with exploring the possibilities that arise from consideration of the black hole as a passageway to another universe or dimension! Rather than being locked in its convictions of how all matter, pulled into a black hole, is crushed in its intense gravity to a "singularity" of immeasurable density, the growing community of quantum physicists is now open to exploring some very exciting possibilities that include multidimensional travel, time travel, and everything in between—and beyond. It opens the scientific world to the greater philosophical question of not only where the passageways lead, but to how, and why, they exist at all.

---

[6] www.newscientist.com/article/dn23611-quantum-gravity-takes-singularity-out-of-black-holes

Perhaps, in my lifetime, I will see science acknowledge the spiritual nature of it all! Should they arrive at the interpretation given to us by the Sirians (and I believe they will), boundless possibilities increase exponentially: that black holes are the astral cords of conscious planetary beings—galaxies, stars, planets—rising in their conscious development to a next level of awareness.

*How I would love to discuss **that** with Stephen Hawking . . . in person!*

Not all the early messages from the Sirian High Council were focused upon the nature of the universe. They also shared several warnings about all kinds of dangers to our societies—things they wished us to be aware of, as guardians of Earth, and of our own lives.

For example, I had never heard of nor seen chemtrails before that information was given to me twenty years ago, and even now—our skies filled with the opacity of the chemical poisons, pathogens, and heavy metal contamination raining down upon us—most people are still in denial. And yet, in the military's documented operation, Weather as a Force Multiplier: Owning the Weather in 2025,[7] *the use of geoengineering is outlined in detail. It is available for anyone willing to investigate how this devastating alteration of the atmosphere and Earth's weather patterns is being perpetrated in the skies of our entire planet.*

Nowhere, not even the highest peaks of the Andes and the Himalayas, is exempt—and this I can attest to personally, as I have been there, and I have seen with my own eyes the chemical ooze pouring from overhead planes. It is not a matter of contrails, or simple water vapor from aircraft exhaust engines, combining with low ambient atmospheric temperatures, to produce cloud-like lines that disappear with the plane's passing.

This poor excuse for an explanation insults our intelligence.

We are witness to relentless spraying of the skies, from planes that are not on a flight pattern from Point A to Point B, a destination orientation—but

---

[7] http://csat.au.af.mil/2025/volume3/vol3ch15.pdf

rather, they weave back and forth, hour after hour, creating tight, grid-like patterns from their emissions. These sprayed chemical trails ooze across the skies and remain for hours, even days, forming a dense haze that is obscuring the sun, and turning the world's beautiful blue skies—everywhere around the world—to dismal grey gloom.

This is no conspiracy theory. It is fact—a reality affecting all of our lives, and every aspect of life upon this Earth.

This military report details the future of weather modification, and its military implications for "the suppression and intensification of weather patterns." The ominous document states:

By 2015, advances in computational capability, modeling techniques, and atmospheric information tracking will produce a highly accurate and reliable weather prediction capability, validated against real-world weather. In the following decade, population densities put pressure on the worldwide availability and cost of food and usable water. Massive life and property losses associated with natural weather disasters become increasingly unacceptable. These pressures prompt governments and/or other organizations that are able to capitalize on the technological advances of the previous 20 years to pursue a highly accurate and reasonably precise weather-modification capability. The increasing urgency to realize the benefits of this capability stimulates laws and treaties, and some unilateral actions, making the risks required to validate and refine it acceptable. By 2025, the world, or parts of it, is able to shape local weather patterns by influencing the factors that affect climate, precipitation, storms and their effects, fog, and near space. These highly accurate and reasonably precise civil applications of weather-modification technology have obvious military implications. This is particularly true for aerospace forces, for while weather may affect all mediums of operation, it operates in ours.

The Council also presented us with information about HAARP, the High Frequency Active Auroral Research Program, which was almost unheard of at that time, and how that system of high powered radio frequency transmitters was operating, in the high frequency band, to essentially "cook the ionosphere," investigating how it could be exploited for purposes of high-tech surveillance, communications, military applications, and weather control.

This highly secretive project was funded by the U.S. Air Force, the Navy, and DARPA (the Defense Advanced Research Projects Agency). Work on the Alaskan facility began in 1993. The Sirians told me about it in 1997—pretty much at its onset, and before even the most die-hard "conspiracy theorists" got on board with what was happening at a U.S. Air Force–owned site on those remote, snow covered plains in Alaska. It was certainly before we could grasp its implications, not only for the United States, nor for the entire North American continent, for that matter—but for the entire globe.

The Council asserted that this black ops HAARP network was an integral part of the secret government's global plan for military weather modification, a plan to essentially weaponize the weather—to include violent earthquakes, tsunamis, and completely unnatural atmospheric conditions, leading to extreme weather and disruption of the ecosystems.

I am sure you will agree that something bizarre is happening to the weather systems around the world: something sinister, or at the very least "unnatural." We are not supposed to connect it to interference of any kind; we are not supposed to notice. The very fact that they are attempting to criminalize the mere mention of "climate change" should speak for itself.

In the first book of the trilogy, The Cosmos of Soul, *channeled from 1996 to 1997, the Council revealed the experimentation under way in secret laboratories, where geneticists were cloning animals, no doubt intent upon or already doing the same with humans. From the cloning of Dolly, the ewe (in 1996), to the disturbing announcement, from the Salk Institute for Biological Studies—made public earlier this year—of their success in creating human/pig hybrid embryos, we are witness to the frightening truth of just where bioengineering intends to steer the course of humanity.*

What are we talking about here: the creation of new, hybrid animal species with humanized brains? Worse yet . . . is it their plan to strip our declining civilization of its intellect, in order to entrap human spirit, mind, and soul in animal bodies, and have us crawling, or walking, on all fours?

What justification is there for these experiments? Shouldn't our scientific communities be working to improve the conditions for life on this planet, rather than genetically altering them? Who is questioning the ethics here? What blind pursuit would have genetic experimenters so driven and determined to create such deviant biological organisms? For what real purpose? And why is there no outrage? Why are we not insisting that the scientific community of biologists and geneticists redirect its focus to that of serving humankind, rather than altering it, to the point that we evolve into laboratory-grown, genetically spliced hybrids?

Are we really to accept, as they are telling us, that the primary purpose for this interference in natural selection is noble: that it is about being able to "grow organs" for our ailing bodies, to be transplanted upon demand?

How unkind is humanity becoming that we are not screaming out against the creation of such creatures, nor are we appalled at the idea of utilizing them for our own, interminable pursuit of extended mortal life? Where is the soul in that? And are we really to believe, despite so-called "ethical restraints" in the scientific community, that there is no cloning of human beings going on in these laboratories? What other freakish hybrids are being created in the underground?

We have only to examine the test laboratories of corporations, producing all manner of consumer products, to recognize how utterly heartless (I dare say "diabolical") researchers can be. I cannot bear to think about it, much less to illustrate the horrific experiments perpetrated on so many animals, often for their entire lifetimes. How can anyone become that anesthetized to suffering?

How much torture helpless, innocent animals are forced to endure, so that humans can wear that extra long lash mascara to enhance their perception of beauty, or smoke their electronic cigarettes to increase their sensate pleasures. By and large, human society turns away, unwilling to look at what we are allowing, in the name of consumption. Surely we are not so naive to believe that this abuse cannot turn on us, where we, in kind, become the laboratory rats of the future.

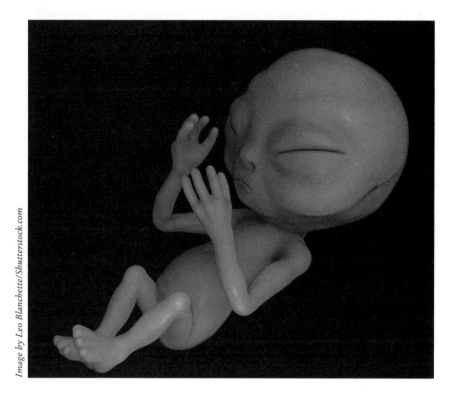

Image by Leo Blanchette/Shutterstock.com

Ask yourself this: are there human beings in cages, adults and children alike, being implanted with or actually growing from alien stem cells, to service Earth-colonizing extraterrestrials in that very same way—for the purpose of creating a hybrid civilization?

A massive collection of alien abduction reports, gleaned from trauma-tized victims for decades now, shares a recurring theme—that this is indeed the case, and that there is an ongoing program, through which human eggs and sperm are joined with alien genetic material in vitro, resulting in an already established community of hybrids—trans-species life forms, of human and alien biology.

You can dismiss this idea as Patricia Cori having read one too many comic books, if you like . . . but do your homework. Thousands of people have reported experiences of abduction—this is public record, and it is available for anyone who wants and is willing to enter the rabbit hole. Many of these traumatized individuals recall having their eggs surgically removed, or their sperm extracted; there are even women who declare to have seen their own babies, hybrid human/Grey alien newborns, in some bizarre alien nursery, where they have been allowed to hold them, just once, never to see them again.

How can anyone survive such a devastating experience?

Personally, I am not sure what would be the more traumatic of the two options: to recall (often only through regression or hypnosis) having had your eggs taken, never to know what will come of them, or to know that your human egg, or sperm, has served to make you the co-creator of a hybrid child, whose destiny you will never share.

There is so much evidence of alien abduction—or at least, there are so many accounts from people believing to have had this experience, working with highly credible psychiatrists and analysts. Can all of these people be deluded, or merely "attention seekers," as they are all too often described? Most of them are traumatized for life—surely there are better ways to find notoriety than to open yourself to criticism, ridicule, and total dismissal for such personal and, in most cases, devastating experiences.

Hybrids, clones, chimeras—all of these deviant applications of biogenetics are altering the very nature of our humanness, and there are very important questions that must at least be asked, if not answered . . . but they are not. Considering the very pressing issues surrounding our runaway population crisis, whereby we are soon to reach eight billion people on this planet, I protest the idea that we need to artificially extend our lives with cloned organs—and of course, I protest in the name of the animals.

Clearly, though, the drug of power that has overtaken this field's masterminds has clouded reason, ethics, and humanity. Geneticists are free to construct their chimeras, experimenting on animals and humans alike, creating their aberrant life forms. The excuse is that we will be able to use these creatures to grow extensions of ourselves, for whatever use we may decide to make of them. To hell with the animals, whose only life experience is to grow hybrid organs, and then to be carved apart—in vivisection, heartless surgery—at harvest time.

One can only imagine how mindlessly their carcasses will be discarded, once the organs are cut out of them: thrown off a research vessel, somewhere in the ocean, or buried in a hazardous waste dump in the earth. Does science care about the consequences of its acts against nature?

What of the consciousness of this manipulated biological matter? We know that every single cell of the body contains memory, and that the mind is not limited to the brain at all. The mind exists in every cell, in every subatomic particle, and in the DNA of all beings—what about that?

Apparently, it just is not a consideration in the laboratory world. Like mindless workers in some car factory, run amok, they will create their spare parts, organs of soulless beings, and sell them, for big profits, to humans in need of replacement parts—to keep their mortal motors running, for as long as they possibly can.

If this arm of the secret government is so determined to extend human life expectancy—here is an idea I'd like to share with the geneticists and the governments who fund them. How about devoting more energy, money, and time to clearing the Earth of the toxins that are destroying the ecosystems around the planet? That would surely extend our lives considerably, just in a reduction of cancer alone. And speaking of cancer, seeing that your intention supposedly is to prolong human life—what say you give us the real cure, or at least allow us, without incrimination, to utilize alternatives, such as cannabinoid oil, to heal ourselves?

What of the development and implementation of valid alternative energy systems? We all know we have them, but that their proliferation is blocked by the oil industry. We know how greatly the quality of all life would be improved if we stopped burning fossil fuels, which would take our civilization to the next level.

You declare that the purpose behind all your genetic tampering is really to provide tissues and organs that will extend human life . . . or to improve the food supply, by altering the DNA of the flora and fauna utilized. Here is a better idea: Why not stop chemtrailing the planet, so that our respiratory systems can heal? Stop genetically modifying our food, so that we once again take wholesome nourishment from that which the earth provides naturally.

Stop creating biological warfare, designed to destroy life.

Stop abusing the Earth.

We do not want your cloned animals, your chimeras, alien/human hybrids, humans with their own replicants, organs, tissues . . . none of it. We want to live in a state of grace, aligned with nature. Anything that interferes with that must come to an end, and soon.

We have the alternative technologies, and the intellect, to heal this planet. What seems to be lacking is the will, from the corporate power structure, and the desire, from the people who have everything to gain from holding it back.

These manic geneticists are not quite ready to present us with their far more advanced achievements (if "achievements" they can be called) in cloning and genetic manipulation . . . but, by the looks of the general ennui from the public regarding the ethical issues surrounding the new human/pig chimera, you can be certain that much more is going to be thrust upon us—day after day. In fact, in these new transmissions, the Council elaborates how, why, and when this reality—already well under way—is being systematically launched into human consciousness, and what our acceptance of the geneticists' deviant designs will mean to our biological evolution.

From intricate explanations of the cosmic forces at work in our solar system and beyond, to warnings about how technology, weaponry, and science would be altering our day-to-day lives, the Speakers of the Sirian High Council have been consistently accurate and boldly prophetic.

There are the doubtful skeptics who rightfully question the source of this information. Is it truly coming to us from the sixth dimension, or is it all a figment of the author's imagination? As before, I reach out to you, skeptics and debunkers alike, and invite you to consider the information presented here for its value, and for the truth inherent within it. In the end, that is what matters. Is it truth to you? Does it touch you, open you, help you to grasp the bigger picture and cope with your immediate world?

I would love to own this wisdom, but I do not. I am no scientist, to be sure, and certainly not an astrophysicist. I am a messenger, a transmitter of sorts, and so many years later—so many books, lectures, speeches later—all I can tell you is that I believe I am one of several people who are using a part of their brain that is wired for ultrasensory perception. It always has been, since the earliest days of my childhood, but it has most definitely accelerated since that fateful time of 1996.

Like cosmic radio receivers, we psychic transmitters manage to reach a frequency that plugs us in to the collective consciousness of all manner of beings from other dimensions, realms, and anything we would include as existing "in the ethers."

But be discerning. Let me declare, once again, that I believe it is the moral and ethical responsibility of any self-proclaimed channel to assure that what comes through, to be shared with the community, is of a higher source, of pure light and untainted wisdom, and not a being or beings seated low in the ethers, awaiting the opportunity to manipulate and infiltrate the body of the one receiving.

This is of the utmost importance and I take the question of that purity of intention very seriously. Very Sirius-ly, indeed.

What comes next? Now that we are witness to the Council's uncannily accurate predictions of the darker agenda, unfolding now, everywhere around us, can we trust their elucidations regarding the ascension of the human collective, and our progression into the light, to be equally precise in scope? We want to rise above the shadow. We pray for intervention, from beyond, to show us how to heal the Earth, and we long to return or move on to a world, or dimension, where love is the common denominator between all conscious beings.

This is our hope, and our longing, and yet—we know we have work to do here. We know that we need to empower that hope with positive action, and a greater community focus on what we can accomplish right here . . . right now. Many of us are well aware that we are starseed, here with a purpose, and a role to play through it all. There will be time enough to return to distant suns, if that is our soul decision. In the meantime, we came into body here, to be part of this monumental shift, to serve Gaia.

We are humans, above all. And this is the right now of our experience.

Still, we long for guidance, comfort, and the reassurance that comes from sources we trust as being anchored in the light. To that end, let us celebrate the return of the Sirian High Council, through the pages you are about to read, with unbridled curiosity, discernment, and the wonder of what appears to be the greatest evolutionary moment of all conscious beings upon this planet, and upon the others of our solar family—where life abounds.

> *We are prepared to offer what insights we can to assist you*
> *in your search for higher truth, but we remind you that it is*
> *from within that you will receive absolute affirmation.*
> *Yours is the task of reaching that truth and turning it outward*
> *for the good of all.*
> *This is your assignment on Planet Earth.*

—Atlantis Rising: The Struggle of Darkness and Light, *Book Two of
the Sirian Revelations trilogy (Berkeley, CA: North Atlantic Books, 2008)*

Image by Argus/Shutterstock.com

2

Declaration of Intent

We, Speakers of the Sirian High Council, hereby declare that it is our express intention to serve and assist you through your transition, and to expound upon unfolding galactic events and their manifestations, as regards their conscious purpose and direction, in which you are either increasingly bewildered or incredibly excited participants.

Always, it is our will to bring to you only that which we intend for your highest personal and collective good, which does include lighting up the dark corners of your mind, those uncomfortable grey areas of your consciousness that you have trained not to look at shadow—but that, denied, only increases their illusory mental and emotional proportions within your mind. Always remember that the awe-inspiring brilliance of a rainbow appears when dark, stormy skies play the background for light, when it dances over and through the dewy moisture of a gentle rain.

There is no place left for the dark masters and their servants to hide: all their caverns are exposed to the light now. You have only to stand above them, as pillars of truth and love, representing the greatness of humanity. Holding firmly to the promontories that jet out over those dark ravines, knowing they can no longer impede you, you are helping to release the negative imprint, so that such immense pain can finally be healed.

There is no more time for denial, for you are racing toward a Golden Age, and your star and the planets are showing you the way to the next dimension, where you will deal with all your karmic debt—to heal, or to know the reward of all good measure—and then move into the light of brighter suns.

There is nothing to gain from holding to any preconceived conviction, freezing your intellect and emotion. But what is needed now, and what we encourage you to place on one plate of the scales of justice and truth, is your finely tuned sense of discernment. On the other, weigh whatever comes into your conscious field: no matter how far-reaching . . . no matter how joyful, or frightening, it may be.

To know truth, without question, requires that you strike a balance and then—and only then—embrace what you have been given. We have always invited you to do that, throughout all of our transmissions, and to exercise the same scrutiny over the teachings and observations of so many self-declared authorities. Trust your own inner knowing and your open heart to weigh, but not to dismiss, other people's perceptions of reality— before you allow or disallow them to affect your own. Then, and only then, will you be more effective in determining what will be beneficial to your own process, and what will not.

Considering all that is being served up to the human race at this time of runaway information, and as the lower astral layers and their malignant entities are being conjured up by the ill-intended and unprepared dabblers of the mystic, you must truly understand that your shields are of the utmost importance. Take note that, most likely, it is not what you want to hear, but what you need to hear, that will be the most relevant to your journey at any given time, but especially now, when you are wading through marshes, to reach clear waters.

Before you read further, we ask that you join us, with the highest of intentions, to recognize, from these transmissions, our dedication to empower you with truth—as we understand it—and to receive the love that carries it to you, through the ethers, from the heart of the sixth dimension, to the one beating in your chest . . . and everywhere in between. Let us all be surrounded in the golden white light, and in this place of union, let the highest good for one and for all be served.

Whatever does not resonate to that standard we invite you to let go. Move past it, and read on. We only ask that you give yourself the opportunity to override any sense of defensive objection to the information, or to put that emotion temporarily aside, so that you can follow us through to the end of this new compendium of revelations, of prophecy for human-kind, through the spectrum of possible realities that you will read here.

Let your conclusions, whether they be synergistic or contrary, follow.

We intend no disruption of your thoughts or unsettling of your emotions, but neither will we paint pictures that we believe would please you, for the sake of stroking your soul. Let it be clear to you, throughout these transmissions, that we are always prepared to sound the wake-up call, and to rouse you from your sleep, if you are still so cuddled up in your distractions that you refuse to open your eyes.

How annoying that incessant bell can be, ringing you awake, when the escapism of sleep and the reverie induced by your detachment from the waking hours can be so much more inviting . . . and comforting. On the other hand, if you are drawn to our messages (which we assume is the case, since you are here), it is surely because you are already well into the awakening, doing your best to cope with your newfound awareness, and with a more universal understanding of the immense changes under way, everywhere around you.

We describe your process as "coping" because we are cognizant of the fact that all aware beings know that mindfulness comes with personal and civil responsibility—and that it is a responsibility not everyone wishes to take on. We celebrate your intention and desire to do just that: to be conscious, determined lightworkers, anchoring love and hope, even in fields of despair and darkness, and to be mindful that all individual acts, and every thought that instigates them, affect the outcome of the entirety.

This means that, to evoke positive change, you must stand solidly against the current of what you are told to believe, for what you know is right—not only for you, but for the universal good.

It means that you will most likely lose people along the way: people who are intimidated by change . . . people who refuse to throw off the covers, and get themselves ready for the work at hand.

It may very well mean that you will be called to sacrifice personal relationships for your ideals: the pursuit of your own soul purpose and the integrity of that objective, over comfort and whatever false sense of security that comes from your unraveling safety nets.

That is nobility, in its highest sense.

Many within your tribes and communities may already have moved on and away, but there will be others, like-minded souls, who will be drawn to your light, the brighter it becomes. We recognize the light of your growing awareness, and feel the immensity of the love that radiates from your heart and soul.

Let go what needs to go, and let in what can serve your readiness for change.

Building upon all that we have shared through to this moment, we are drawn to illuminate those cosmic energies, in varying states of dissolution, reorganization, and materialization, that are particularly relevant to you, as primary guardians of Gaia—an honor you share with the Great Whales and the Dolphin Beings, who are doing everything within their power to hold the harmonics of your great oceans in balance.

To attempt to describe the transformation of the entire solar system, the body of Ra, is, by any measure, mammoth in scope, and, as you, we are distant observers of its pirouetting energy: matter and spirit, dancing center stage to your star in the heavens. But, unlike you, and because we are witness to events from a higher dimension, we do have perspectives that exceed your current reach. To make them meaningful to you, hopefully transformational in scope, and in terms that are relative to your current three-dimensional reality base (your mind's perceived anchor), is the real challenge before us.

Hence, we ask you to bear with us—to bend, and be malleable . . . and to reach, and be daring—as we focus our communal lens, so that we may bring to you our considerations upon the most salient information relative to this point in "time," and so that we can organize our thoughts in order to reach you, by conveying their essence through the heart and mind of our transmitter, Trydjya of Antares, whose electromagnetic receptivity and conscious intent align with ours.

Of all the planets, moons, and configurations bearing life in your solar system, we are focused primarily upon you, *Homo sapiens,* reawakening, but that does not mean we are any less attentive to, or concerned about, the entire biosphere of life upon the Earth. We do have open communication with the Cetaceans, for there are Elders here—the Q'iquoq'i—who sit on the Sirian High Council, whom you will have encountered in their messages to you, a short time ago.[8] The Q'iquoq'i monitor all planetary and lunar waters—not only the oceans of Earth . . . connecting with their fellows on planets and dimensions throughout the Cosmos. In essence, what we are saying here is that where there is water, there is a life form that holds that body of water to a certain rhythm, a certain song. That life form is one of myriad species that conforms with your perception of the Great Whales and the Mighty Dolphin Beings.

We are always concerned that we be as concise as nonhumanly possible, for, often, our observations are so far-reaching and contradictory to the status quo as to appear implausible to you. We understand that you must stretch yourselves to grasp what is yet unproven, and rarely discussed, in your realm of experience. Then again, what is "unproven" describes most of the universe! The task before us is to bridge that gap, with words that are relevant to your own perception, about subjects that cover an immeasurable field of expression and activity—reflections of perpetual change and evolutionary shifts, across the Cosmos. The enormity of this galactic shift has already begun to open countless possible realities to you all . . . realities that are intangible, perhaps, but no less substantial than what you can touch, see, and hear.

Our thoughts, made crystalline through the written word, can only be significant and meaningful to you, as individuals and as a community, if they reach you. Do we touch you, bringing you to a clearer sense of what is happening around you, and helping you to harness your energies? How can we serve to help you contribute to the collective, in ways that raise the

---

[8] Patricia Cori, *Before We Leave You: Messages from the Great Whales and the Dolphin Beings* (Berkeley, CA: North Atlantic Books, 2011).

vibrations around you—to then send them rippling out into the rich and fertile subconscious of human awareness, where they can be seeded and brought to bloom?

These considerations underlie all of our messages, and they are a clear reflection of our intention at all times, throughout every moment of our interactions with you, through the channel . . . through these words.

Our messages are only effective keyholes, in the iron doors of locked minds, if the prophecies and information contained within them either come to pass (as with the first Sirian Revelations), or if they can be integrated into your existing knowledge base—again, as individuals and as societies. If not, the information shared here will be lost in translation. We say this to remind you, although you are already well aware, that the greater body of human beings is still shut down, its back to the looking glass, and you will be tested, even ridiculed, for bringing new ideas into an old, tattered matrix.

But . . . do it anyway.

We are determined to cut through the dogma of conditioned belief structures and, yet, retain enough essential truth that you can be moved to challenge authority, and to see beyond the walls of its dictates and false illusions. These are words that need to contain elements of scientific deduction, in its highest forms, and yet not be limited to its dictates and observations. They must be inspired, but still grounded enough in your experience that they can make sense to you, so that you can take them to heart and apply them to your own lives—and to visions of what will come. Else, they are no more than wisps of consciousness blowing in the wind, dissipating into the silence of all that is unspoken and never shared.

That is a challenge that we, representatives of the Sirian High Council, take to heart and soul. It is our wish to help you to see through the low-lying clouds that blind you, at times, disorienting you from your path, and as much as possible, to serve as a lantern that will help guide you to clear skies ahead.

So, be patient with us. We share all of these heartfelt considerations in order that you understand how deeply we hold your progression to the light of integrity and truth, as we understand it, and to feel how we long for you to find peace—once again. Always remember, through you—through one person—we are addressing the collective, which embraces a wide spectrum of belief systems and levels of perception. Set your mind free, and let your thoughts and the wonder of all possibility traverse the ethers, to be shared by those who resonate with your accelerating pace and perceptions.

For some, we may be overly complicated in our approach and terminology; for others, we may not be daring enough! We are well aware that, above all, we must be always vigilant in our intention to assist, but not to interfere, and to scrupulously honor the journey of every sovereign being, and the progression of all humanity.

Hopefully we have found the middle ground, where all who are listening can hear.

That is our express intention.

Let it be so received.

3

Greetings from Satais

In the name of light beings and loving souls from all realms and dimensions that comprise the infinite Cosmos, and honoring the sovereignty of all attuned to our missives, through these written words, as we honor the integrity of our devoted transmitter, Trydjya of Antares, we greet you, beloved Children of Gaia.

We are three primary Speakers of the Sirian High Council, coming to you from the midway of the sixth dimension, specifically from the heightened emanations of our ascended star, Satais (identified by your astronomers as Sirius B), which holds resonance at this dimensional frequency, to which we will also refer to as "density," intermittently—for both describe aspects of our unified field of experience.

Of the three sister stars that comprise our multidimensional, interstellar family, Sothis (Sirius A) is the only one that remains anchored in the universe of matter, and we are quite certain that you are familiar with this star, for it is a close neighbor, although it may not be perceived as "close" from your earthly viewpoint. In more far-reaching, galactic terms, it is indeed a local relative to your own sun, Ra—approximately eight of your "light years" away. For reasons of that proximity, as well as of its immense luminosity, it is most likely to be perceived as the brightest of stars in your night sky.

Were your own sun, Ra, destined to remain in its physical body, where it holds a rather remote position in relationship to the center of the Milky Way galaxy, Sothis would appear even more brilliant centuries from now . . . for it is moving closer to you. From its position, sitting low on your horizon and shining even brighter its captivating bluish light, its energies would be felt even more powerfully than they have across time on Earth, when Sothis was so revered by the ancients, whose lives were guided by the heliacal rising of the star—and because so many of them (like you) were starseed from Sirius.

However, as you will glean from our communications, and incorporating that which you have already experienced as your own intuitive interface with rather inexplicable mutations of time and place, you have very possibly reached that point of recognition whereby you understand that your solar system has already actively begun its ascension process: from the constraints of the physical universe, onto more refined levels of energy.

Whether you are aware of the anomalies springing forth from this transition, or whether you are still distracted by the illusions (constraints of space and time that give form to the life in which you have immersed yourselves) that give you a very solid sense of identity, you are nonetheless slipping in and out of your present density, catching an occasional wave of the fourth dimension as it washes across the terra firma of your perception. If you are aware of those moments, and where they take you, you are no doubt experiencing a conscious wavelength that is very different from that of most people around you. In a sense, you have set sail, feeling the shifts in the currents, swaying with the pull of the tide, and knowing that you are still not fully emerged in the deep waters of altered reality—but that you are most definitely headed there.

In a nonspatial sense, you will be moving closer to the ascended stars of Sirius, closer to us, in ways you may not yet understand, and leaving Sothis, Sirius of the material universe, behind.

You are the privileged to experience this event within the framework of your own lifetime. No matter how rocky the waters, always remember that you do know where safe harbor lies, and that you can always find your way back in, whenever you feel lost on the high seas.

The third Sirian star, Anu (Sirius C), ascended to the fourth dimension, and has yet to move beyond it. This has so much to do with its interference in your progression (described in our work entitled *Atlantis Rising: The Struggle of Darkness and Light*) via the planet, Nebiru, which was expelled from that celestial transition, and left to roam dark space. If you are curious to delve deeper into our understanding of this planet's effect upon you, or to consider the celestial mechanics that were involved, we invite you to read that earlier missive, for we do not wish to repeat ourselves . . . but rather to progress with fresh perspectives on how that involvement is changing, in the wake of Earth's acceleration.

There you will surely find answers, or at least food for contemplation, for how these two specific stars (Anu, the Sirian star, and Ra, your own solar deity) interact. More specifically, you will access earlier information on how one planet of that system could so dramatically affect your own—and how it still clutches the Earth for its very survival.

We, the ascended of Satais, are no longer in body; instead, we exist as pure consciousness, a state of being that you often do achieve in astral flight, and in the dream state—whether you recall the experience upon waking, or not. Yet, you have such difficulty understanding how any one being could possibly exist as an aspect of the collective consciousness—without corporeal form and without ego. But we do understand physicality, because we were once physical, like you, and, in that context, we conformed to the laws of physics of that plane—laws that are far more elaborate and far-reaching in scope than you might ever imagine.

Despite the dogmatism of established earth physics, those laws, which include perfected displays of cosmometric proportion, and the interdependency of every single element of the greater Unity, are certainly not all understood by your scientific communities. They have still not identified elements, chemicals, and so much more that govern the mechanical universe. By the very nature of those missing pieces, one can only conclude that earth science is, at its worst, erroneous. At its best, it is incomplete—and therefore inconclusive. Remember that . . . when you consider, or are so told, that only scientific proof can confirm any given axiom or hypothesis.

Can you imagine, then, the difficulty the collective scientific mind is currently encountering, attempting to grasp what physical laws could possibly govern nonphysical dimensions that somehow co-exist with, but are not comprised of, matter? Old laws that have been ineffectual in describing the workings of your own planet certainly cannot claim governance over the intricacies of the greater celestial dynamic. They simply do not work unilaterally, and therefore can only apply, at best, to a very limited scope of the universal picture.

Take, for example, the question of gravity. It is one of the most significant forces holding sway over the universe of matter, and yet, the nature of gravity remains a perpetual conundrum for your physicists, who are still trying to figure out how and why everything celestial adheres, in some miraculous bond, in proportions that allow for sovereign experience within celestial unities, such as solar systems. It is the mysterious glue that binds, holding galaxies intact, just as it holds the oceanic sheath that surrounds the Earth attached to your own planet. Do you think about that? It is the overriding force that allows you and all the other creatures to walk the ground beneath your feet, so that you do not simply float off into the atmosphere and disintegrate, forever lost . . . in space dust.

Amongst so many theoretical applications to the study of gravity, quantum science is involved in a quest to determine whether it exists at the subatomic level, and how it would be represented in the interaction of electrons, protons, and neutrons, and yet-to-be-identified elements of the subatomic field.

However, you spiritualists already know, of course, that it must be so — there must be a gravitational force present in the subatomic interchange. You do not need scientific proof of this reality, because you already understand that, from the subatomic to the mega-galactic, there is one axiom that holds true for all existence—and that is, without question, that the microcosm is the exact reflection of the macrocosm, and vice versa: "As above, so below; and as below, so above."

In other words, whatever exists in the universe of matter, and however its elements interact, they do so, in the very same way, in the microcosmic, subatomic world—for they are one and the same. Hence, if gravity is operating on Earth and throughout the physical universe, it must be equally expressed in the subatomic field, and—by the nature of that presence—you can only deduce that it is performing in the same way, for the same purpose, within and around your own bodies.

You, living beings who dwell upon a sphere in space, experience yourselves in a form that adheres to the rules of science to an extent, somewhere in the middle, between the microscopic and the mega-galactic. You, too, are made of those same elements, interacting in the same exact proportions and manifestations. The missing pieces, regarding the consciousness that orchestrates all life and all energy, form the pervasive mystery puzzle that eludes (in varying degrees) empirical knowledge.

That is not to say that your scientific researchers and theoretical physicists are still groveling, trying to find their way in the dark. We do not intend that, not by any means, for we do honor their contributions . . . insofar as those efforts are for the greater good of all beings, and just as long as they never depend upon the suffering of living beings, as a means to justifying their experimental ends.

From the time when scientific hierarchies on Earth invented their first electron microscopes, to present-day use of highly sophisticated neutron microscopic technology, and the highly unstable Large Hadron Collider,[9] they have been capable of exploring how the subatomic universe is truly organized. As a by-product, and through countless experiments, they have come to recognize how atomic and subatomic fields reflect and react to consciousness, for they can identify change in their lenses, as samples being examined react to being observed.

No matter how sterile or objective the experiment, they can never isolate the subject from the observer, as consciousness interacts, shares, and responds, in kind. That interaction, the relationship between conscious mind and subatomic matter, is undoubtedly the greatest discovery of all, even though its importance and meaning still escape the primary focus of their attention.

No attempt to isolate an experiment from the one viewing it has ever been completely effective, and it never will be; therefore, no absolute objectivity can be gleaned from any given test. How frustrating, and yet, how very fascinating it must be for science to recognize the interconnectedness of consciousness and the power of the mind upon matter—from within its structural limitations, attempting purely analytical definition. It is a great step forward for empirical knowledge, as it acknowledges that

---

[9] The world's largest particle accelerator, activated by CERN in 2008 in Switzerland.

every living thing is consciously aware, on some level, and that nothing can be completely isolated from the universal field of conscious awareness.

The more adventurous theorists are ready to take a giant leap, where they hope to discover and identify the "god code" within DNA, bringing them closer to the ultimate understanding of how all matter—regardless how dense or how dark its substance—is a reflection of the Cosmic Soul.

Until that point, when earth-based science embraces the sacred wisdom that contains the one absolute truth underlying all manifestation—that it is conscious intention that designs everything that appears physical in nature—they will only be skirting the truth, like dancers in the flicker of a campfire's light.

As you will glean from reading this material, and applying what you already believe you know about the multiverse, it would be more accurate to define the sixth dimension as a "refined density"—a place or, better yet, an aspect of the Cosmic Unity. It is far more subtle than the one you are experiencing as the 3D framework, from which you believe you are connecting to other-worldly information, in the very words you are reading now.

Because this density is so much more refined, energetically, than the realm of matter and its physical manifestations, it is not subject to those laws, which we have suggested are incomplete and inconclusive. Science, itself, admits its own limitations. And yet, it is because of those laws that your conventional scientific community would prefer to dismiss the idea of multidimensional communication altogether, as they perpetually reiterate the mantra: "If it does not adhere to the laws of physics, it isn't real."

Would that not be defined as an incongruity?

Fortunately, you do have this generation of scientific pioneers, the quantum physicists, who are pushing the preconceived boundaries of science to new heights, and they are a most exquisite reflection of humankind reaching higher, seeking to know the formerly "unknowable." They are recognizing how these laws are not only incomplete and antiquated, but how they are inadequate for the twenty-first century.

If laws cannot define how the physical universe works, then clearly, they are even more irrelevant to what lies beyond that level of experience. New theories, inspired by the Age of Information, and the heightened frequencies of your place in space, are propelling science in new directions. Quantum theorists are reexamining ideas considered "heretical" from the constricted past, developing new and fascinating approaches to the questions of a quantum omniverse, and challenging their contemporaries who still adhere to the limitations of empirical knowledge and proof-through-analysis.

They are coming so much closer to an understanding of what spiritualists have always known: that nothing that exists in the Cosmos of Soul can be confined to any given set of rules, or parameters, that deny the presence of consciousness, will, and intent. The next step, recognizing how it is consciousness that creates it all, awaits them in the halls of "higher" education, which have nothing to do with academia, and everything to do with soul, reaching higher, searching for truth.

What if we told you that the physical universe is merely a holographic projection of conscious creation, as opposed to your perception of other dimensions being the projection, and matter being the reality? Or, if we explained how your soul anchor is really not found in the density of your physical life, and in your perception of the manifested world of Earth, but rather, that it is in the light of eternal being, a multidimensional sequence of universal DNA that spans the entirety of the Cosmos, from which you created that world, and that body, to begin with? More challenging still is the precept that you created not only that one reality, or framework, where you believe you reside at this moment, but countless others, where you exist as simultaneous versions of yourself.

We will share more with you that regards your omnipresence in parallel universes and simultaneous reality; you have our commitment to elaborate that in considerations and observations that will soon follow.

You know, deep within you, that your every thought, and all the genetic information that is reflected through your conscious experience, are simply extensions of the one mind that is laced across and throughout all existence. Yet, one cannot help but wonder: Where does the core of my existence lie? What is the truest, purest reality? Are we all an endless reflection of consciousness, bouncing its self-aware reflection around and around, in some cosmic hall of mirrors?

We hear the questions that all conscious physical beings cannot help but ask themselves—not that we claim for a moment to know everything there is to know of existence.

What is real and unreal?

What is truth, and what is an illusion?

When will we be able to discern the difference?

Until that glorious hour of our soul return, when we finally merge back into Source, the light of Creation, how could we ever know the purpose and the meaning of all that exists? We, Sirians, are constantly climbing the spiral of light, as are you, and like you, we are just as eager to discover more of the divine plan of existence. We only know as much as is our conscious capacity to perceive and understand, and that is a wealth of wisdom that grows, changes, and blossoms with every step we take. We are not based in desire for knowledge; rather, we are filled with wonder at the process of discovering the way of the immortal soul, with all its bends and turns, peaks and valleys.

We, Sirians, find great peace in that, for what would life, the journey of the soul, be . . . without wonder? We believe, and it has been our experience, that it is not being there, the "arrival," that matters. It is the "getting there" that fascinates and perpetuates our desire to move forward.

These very deep, existential questions are hardly new to human civilization, or to any other consciously aware life forms across the universe, including some who exist beside you, as Earth residents.

You may not consider animals intelligent enough to possess self-awareness, much less to exhibit curiosity about, or to ponder, the meaning of their lives. Surely life forms exist for more reasons than just to serve humanity, with no other purpose than to fill your landscape with colors, and provide you with entertainment, food, and their servitude. If you see life that way, you are fooled, for many species are self-aware and capable of such contemplations.

All beings have their own higher purpose, one that is served by their existence, individually, and collectively, as entire species. You only have to think of the bees, and the great work they do, pollinating immense fields of flora, to recognize how important even the smallest creature is to the entirety. There are the Great Whales and the Dolphin Beings, who hold the music and the rhythms of the oceans in balance. You have remarkable sea dwellers, many of them performing the unimaginable feat of illuminating the dark and deep oceans; they are—in every sense—not of your world. No less aware are the great apes, who have incredible knowledge to share with you—if only they spoke the language that could break through to the human mind . . . or better yet, if only human beings could communicate as effectively, and telepathically, as they do.

There are so many more overlooked wisdom keepers in your animal kingdoms, and they are complex, intelligent, and aware. From the smallest insects, who show you the synchronicities and mutual benefit of community, such as bees and ants, to wild elephants, who hold rituals to assist the souls of their tribal members when they pass over the rainbow bridge to the spirit kingdom, extraordinary intelligence and awareness permeate the biological expanse of your world.

Across the millennia, humankind has searched the stars to give meaning to life and to receive guidance and direction, so very often overlooking the wisdom encoded into every living being that surrounds them, on every level. You created gods and demons to define forces that were beyond your comprehension, always seeking to understand man's role in the greater scheme of all things.

In the peaks of civilization, such as those of early Atlantis, Egypt, Sumeria, Lemuria, and others buried in the ambiguity of forgotten history, the questions of man's place in the universe, and of a greater understanding of the forces at play on Earth, were answered, in part, by the ancients' contact and interaction with several extraterrestrial races who, in many ways, contributed to Earth's development.

Extraterrestrial exploration of your planet goes back far before *Homo sapiens* was seeded there. Their visitations, and clues to what they have contributed in those times, have been reflected in the true historical record—at least what remains of it. It is in the prehistoric glyphs carved into remote caves, and buried in the hidden books of those who preferred to have you see historical events through their own eyes, with their own religious, political, and racial agendas. Even today, with your probing and the proliferation of information, much of what you are privileged to and are embracing as truth of this enigma has been distorted through misinterpretations of those who do not truly understand, or whose agenda it is to be certain that you never do.

All great civilizations, and we speak of those that have flourished on planets beyond the Earth, as well as those contained within Gaia's own experience, share three common existential pursuits. These are, without exception: the exploration of the immortal soul; a quest to understand the god code that is laced throughout all life, everywhere, in Creation; and a conscious respect for and interaction with all nature that defines the environment—to include animals, insects, plants, the mineral kingdom, and the air itself.

It must be noted that, just like yours, all civilizations decline rapidly once they replace their worship of nature, and the love of every living thing, with the ego inherent in states of separation from the divine, which inevitably devolves into greed, violence, crime against the "other," war, and, eventually, the complete downfall of society. Add to that the encroachment of technology—based on the processing and manipulation of untold quantities of data, rather that the love of Creation, and it is no wonder that entire species are becoming extinct, where once they thrived in their own planetary harmonics.

As you, the awakening, are well aware, Earth finds itself in a dichotomy, reflected in the incredibly polarized range of human desire, expectation, and contemplation. You are at once at the highest peaks and lowest valleys, in this time and in your experience of life there, and this is very particular to your contemporary civilization—a world in utter confusion and chaos—reflective of your own metamorphosis, and the phases through which you are passing.

This unparalleled evolutionary catalyst has never before occurred on any planetary field within your solar system, nor at any other time upon the Earth, and we implore you to understand how it is affecting the entirety, the planetary body, just as it is redefining your personal and individual relationships to Earth, and to the stars.

Whereas those civilizations born of humankind's heightened awareness may have devotedly contemplated a multiverse, aided even by influences from beyond, they did not live it. They could not know, as you are coming to know, what it meant to be shifting out of the physical universe, and ascending to another density—not as a personal experience or pursuit of one's own spiritual journey, but, rather, as a planetary body, refining itself to be attuned and resonant with another dimensional field, in a constantly shifting, mutating multiverse of varying degrees of light and consciousness.

When you are filled with trepidation, and so overwhelmed by the orchestrated darkness that appears to dominate life there, in the confusion of your world, remember what we are describing for you here. Remember how truly blessed you are to be alive, to experience something that no human being ever to walk the Earth has experienced before.

No one. No illuminated priest of mighty Atlantis, nor Egyptian Pharaoh . . . no great philosopher, no scientific genius, and not even any corporeal extraterrestrial visitor from anywhere that could be defined as being from across time and space, could ever have experienced what you are just beginning to experience now. You are slipping into a realm where all the rules of the physical universe no longer apply . . . and where time, your measure of existence, no longer exists.

There is no moment in Gaia's own history when that kind of galactic shift in the communal experience occurred. You have come to the turning point in existential no-man's-land, in a sense, and only others, such as we, who have come to it before you, know what it means to look back upon the physical universe from another dimension.

True, you may have had out-of-body experiences, and glimpses from dreams and altered states, but again, we are speaking to the entirety: many different people, at different phases of their experience. Some of you are much more attuned than others, and you are seeing more clearly what others cannot yet see. You are blessed, through the wonder of your place in the multiverse of possibility, to see beyond the collective fear of mortal annihilation . . . and so are you the blessing itself, for others who find hope in your visions.

How can they not?

You are shining light into darkness, love into fear, and more, you are helping others to contemplate their own immortality.

That awareness is a first step on a path you will walk in the very near future, which we will refer to as "the days ahead," allowing for poetic license that does not speak of days, or years, but as the unfolding of experience.

Here, in the sixth dimension, we are not subject to the illusions of matter, nor do we experience separation, where bodies, walls, and other boundaries appear to define reality, creating isolation one from the other. Those three-dimensional illusory fields create a distortion of reality, and it is from within that distortion that you find yourselves at this point, while you struggle to grasp the existence of light-bodied beings, souls in transition, and heavenly orbs that have ascended to higher planes.

It is our charge, as it is our karmic responsibility, to communicate relevant cosmic events and considerations, involving interplanetary developments, to all intelligent life forms residing across your entire solar system. We believe that, if we can facilitate your understanding of a future where you progress out of this illusory field, you will be far better equipped to deal with the disharmonies that are currently rocking your personal lives and shaking your world.

For reasons that go back to the very time of the Great Experiment (the seeding of *Homo sapiens* on Earth, over one hundred thousand years ago), we are quite specifically centered on and concerned with the evolution of your species there, on Planet Earth—the "communication station" of your star's family of celestial beings. We feel great concern for the planet itself, and for every living being upon it—but it is you, and the spirit essence of your planet, Gaia, that are our primary focus. That said, we cannot separate your process from the entirety of all that surrounds your place in space, and all that is unfolding across that field of experience.

Your sun is a stellar body in extreme transition, at all planetary stations, and including the natural satellites that orbit them: moons, asteroids, and all the minute particles and microcosmic forms that filter through that interstellar space.

All are conscious; all are accelerating.

We embark upon this work by merging with our transmitter, Trydjya of Antares, on this most auspicious Earth Day (August 4, 2016) of planetary alignments, when five celestial beings in your solar field—those you refer to as Mercury, Venus, Mars, Jupiter, and Saturn—are aligned in perfect proportion from your setting solar deity, your sun, Ra. From Earth, you can observe this rather extraordinary display on the ecliptic plane, forming a straight line across the sky. This rare array is visible to stargazers at all points, and from every continent on your planet.

We understand that you will be reading these thoughts and contemplations many moons from now, allowing for completion of a manuscript—the process of giving proper form to a collection of transmissions, and then making it available to you. But it is our wish for you that, as you read it, you still can recall your gaze upon this profound summer sky, one that provided such an inspiring vision that, even as you read these words, you will be capable of recalling the splendor of such galactic scenery in your night skies.

Those of you who were paying attention to the bejeweled canopy overhead at that time (which actually is our "time," at this transmission) surely remember bearing witness to an exceptional phenomenon of synchronized celestial physics. Or perhaps you will simply remember feeling the pull and sway of those celestial influences upon your individual physical, emotional, and mental bodies. We invite you to ponder how, similarly, conscious, intelligent beings on other planets in your family of spheres also observed that sacred sight, perhaps even contemplating your own planet's position—relative to others.

We assure you that, across your solar body, untold numbers of conscious beings are looking back upon the Earth, wondering, feeling, and contemplating what the blue-green planet means to the overall question of life beyond their borders . . . and to their own survival and evolution.

If only you will release yourselves from the hypnotic, addictive control of your proliferating electronic devices, which are effectively altering your brain waves. Take yourselves out into the cool dark of evening, when suns of so many worlds shine through the lattice of material space, where you will be reminded of how multitudinous are the possibilities of life, everywhere beyond your station.

From our perspective, as discarnate beings holding light in the sixth dimension, we are capable of gazing upon any point on the space-time continuum, just as effortlessly as you might look upon a gigantic computer screen. We are free to observe that layer of reality, the physical universe, in specific quadrants, so vast is its breadth.

We are capable of observing any point on the space-time continuum, but we are no longer able to hold resonance there. We cannot adhere to form.

But we hear the music.

Emanating from your precious orb, and from those that comprise your solar body, to the remotest stars, where, there too, countless planetary bodies are teeming with intelligent life, is divine music. The universe—a constant, breathtaking array of celestial harmonics—plays the perpetual song of Creation, in one monumental, unending symphony.

It is of intelligent design. It is the sound of consciousness unfolding, in complex and yet such simple designs, and you are the musicians . . . just as you are the audience that listens.

At this moment in galactic "time," this cosmic symphony is playing the opus of your sun's imminent passage out of the material universe; and every living being, upon all those celestial bodies that adhere to your solar field, is contributing to a very specific melody: the Music of the Spheres, music that is preparing to deliver your sun onto a higher plane.

In ways that may make sense to you, ascension is the reverse process of being birthed from spirit essence into the density of the material realm.

Always, in the progression of souls, there is this transition from states of being that involves passing through the tunnels, tubes, or gateways that exist for that express purpose.

When planetary bodies align in such brilliant array, you are looking at a sort of sheet music, the depiction of celestial chords being played across the energy fields of your solar system. What we wish to impress upon you is that your thoughts, actions, and conscious awareness of who you are, and of what you have come to do in this physical life, are so very much a part of that.

Please hold this thought close to your hearts: you are not merely observing, you are playing the music—contributing to Gaia's own music, and in turn, playing a galactic chord, within the Music of the Spheres.

If you can understand that, you can feel so much more integrally your own vibratory involvement in Earth's progression.

And of course, racing across the horizon, in ships that are not that far more advanced than those in development at secret locations on Earth, away from public scrutiny, there are physical beings: extraterrestrial visitors and watchers. Plenty are the craft whizzing about there, in and around your atmosphere. They are boldly visible to those who are looking and, moreover, to those who are open to seeing them. Despite the interference and confusion created by electromagnetic weapons and satellite devices, holographic distortions, and your own governments' experiments, you still can see them.

Sightings are reported from one side of the globe to the other, when you are really paying attention to what is going on overhead, and when, of course, your skies are clear enough for you to penetrate the cloud layers, and the gauze of unnatural, sprayed chemical shields. Not all ships in the night are of extraterrestrial navigation, for your own sophisticated and secret craft are proliferating, but these are still far from achieving the extraordinary maneuvers that come with overriding gravity—or redefining space.

Navigators of exoplanetary alien craft, whether of the light or darker intentions, are observing the Earth, weighing the harmonics of the planet's emissions, and watching your societal behaviors. They are charting the geophysical alterations of the surface, and mutations of the atmosphere, just as you have begun to do with planets that lie within your reach.

Needless to say, however, and as you no doubt can imagine, extraterrestrials studying Earth are more concerned with the pressing matter at hand: humanity's thermonuclear capacities, and your absolute inability to manage that force responsibly. They are observing space wars technology and weapons being positioned in your outer atmosphere (in preparation for what your own military intends to be an imminent war in your galactic quadrant), to determine how great a risk you are now, and what you soon can become, unchecked, to your neighboring planets.

Measuring the radiation that already emanates from your planet, the more spiritually evolved of these space voyagers are also weighing the ecological deterioration of the Earth against the probable reality that will send it careening through the astral cord of your sun, when it transits out of the physical universe.

In the tether of planets aligning to make the transition, Earth is strategically positioned to draw the inner two planets through the stellar cord. Were it to be expelled, due to its declining energy fields, it could take those planets with it. This is one (but surely not the **only**) reason why watchers of Earth changes are hovering, studying what you cannot deny is a civilization of war and significant destruction. Moreover, they are analyzing the weakening atmospheric conditions of the planet's auric field, examining the devastating decline of your oceanic environments, and determining how advanced is Earth's dis-ease.

As always, there are other conscious entities, such as we, who are observing you from other dimensions. We do not need craft, nor do we need to buzz around your space, for we are experiencing you from another density, so close you might almost touch us, if we were in form. But we are not.

We are energy . . . conscious energy.

That energy permeates the light that surrounds you, and our love filters through all the illusions that divide you from each other, from the Earth, and from Spirit itself. We, too, study your planet's health and well-being, but we do this from a place of knowing that it is a work in progress. That is, we do not observe, fearing the outcome. We know that you are capable of correcting the imbalances, and that the nature of that disharmony is, in a very urgent sense, a call to action.

The extreme is taking you to resolution, and that is a brilliant thing to watch. You may not yet understand how, but we can see that you are not going to allow your world to be so devastated that it will not proceed into the higher dimensions.

So many lightworkers are taking the reins now, guiding the course of change.

Silent but never absent, we Sirians, representatives of several well-integrated multidimensional civilizations of the Cosmic Unity, have been quietly observing this difficult, but quite exhilarating, Earth transition, out of the constraints of the third dimension. Your circumstances have positioned us now to share with you what we perceive as the subsequent phases of your personal and planetary evolution.

Through the din of immense turmoil, and the confusion that challenges your existence and (we will go so far as to say) your very sanity, we do hear your implorations: "Where are you?" "Why won't you help us?" "When will you come to save us?"

Despite the waves of compassion that stir within us, we do feel compelled to remind you, as we have, time and time again, that you do not need to be saved. That conviction, that only someone or something from beyond your realm and beyond your capabilities can save you and your planet, effectively delays your progression. It is vibrationally opposed to Gaia's own immense ability and innate intention to survive and flourish, no matter what is thrown at her, in this time of extreme abuse and neglect: not only from the mind-numbing methodologies of despots who rule over you, but from the very human race itself.

It is, in essence, absolutely contrary to that which most of you desire for your future, and to that which you wish to create, as guardians of the planetary world upon which you reside.

It should make sense to you that, if you can be convinced of the coming of a savior, one who will override the "evil" that lurks within or around you, you will wait. Passive and disempowered, you will wait for that occurrence, never fully owning the clear and present truth that all seven and one-half billion of you, *Homo sapiens*, are meant to be the true caretakers of the planet—and that you possess the collective power to override the few who still lord over you through military, technological, and economic tyranny.

For the sake of your planetary deity, Gaia, and all the living beings who share her glorious landscapes with you, we ask you to release yourselves, once and forever, from that disempowering mindset: "a savior cometh . . ."

Know, without a shadow of doubt, that you are indeed the ones who have come to save—or rather, to assist—the Earth, and that **you** are the ones you are waiting for. So, stop waiting, and take action now, everywhere and any way you can, to bring light to darkness.

Look around you. Do not be afraid, or resistant to examining what is happening, in the world in which you live. You do not have to participate or commit emotionally. You can observe with objectivity and balanced detachment. While cruelty and destruction appear to be the order of every day, something far greater is unfolding . . . and the awakening amongst you know it.

It is visceral.

You can feel it prickling your skin, the charge coursing through your neural highways, your blood, and your sensors: the quickening.

It is not that the texture of the world has changed to fit your vision of a "higher" dimension—as you understand your ascension process to be. Somehow, the enormity of the Great 2012 Shift was not tangible nor "cinematic" enough to get your full attention; in fact, for most of you it was elusive . . . and so subtle, you may not even have noticed.

Things still appear to be the same—so very three-dimensional—in so many ways. But they are not, and you, the awakening, have begun now to see and feel the difference. Many of you are now experiencing time shifting or even disappearing, in a sense, to where you are confused about what is transpiring and what is happening to you. You experience an event that appears to be absolutely "real," but that has not really occurred. When it happens the next day or later, exactly as you experienced it, you can easily question your sanity.

One could describe this phenomenon as the "slipping bands" of space-time, like some loose conveyor belt in a factory. Or rather, that you are moving from one time line to another . . . but this is erroneous.

You are simply attuning to another frequency, where time does not exist.

You are evolving to a frequency that resonates with the quintessential vibratory essence of the fourth dimension. Through the chaos that abounds there, on Earth, where you can only wonder if your planet will survive the madness, you are unquestionably beginning to segue into the fourth dimension.

As you progress even more, or shall we say, as you attune to the frequencies of four-dimensional awareness, you will be experiencing timelessness altogether. There will be no measure of what day or hour or minute it is, or what just occurred, as a result of any given time frame. You will be faced with your role in these events with bewilderment, until you finally acclimatize, recognizing how what you are leaving behind—that sense of linear time—is nothing but an illusion.

Will we ever be able to successfully describe this state of consciousness to you, while you are still subject to the confines of the third dimension? It is most unlikely, for, although you are emerging from it, you are still physically bound to it. But it is now, twenty of your years since we first spoke to you of the "no-time," that you are in that state of transition where, if you are not already consciously experiencing the fourth dimension, you are at least ready for it to unveil its curious nature to your eager minds and spirits.

We celebrate that curiosity—that contemplation that comes from the higher self that searches for the meaning of all existence. This is the nobility of soul, and we resonate to it.

We feel we can touch you, when you reach out. Won't you take our hand and let us guide you, from a very particular vantage point, through this last difficult walk past the Desert Days of your struggling civilization, to the high ground that awaits?

We are here for you. Whether you perceive our love as an outstretched hand, or whether you feel the signature vibratory frequency that emanates from our union, we are here, by your side.

Loving you, we are watching you push through the roadblocks . . . the barriers . . . the walls that have been used to divide you, or to deter you, completely, from your path.

Hold steady, for you are on course, on your way to the clearing—just a little bit further, past the last hurdle.

4

What of the Stars?

Over the great expanse of more than one hundred thousand years of human existence that corresponds with the hour of your seeding as *Homo sapiens,* through to the present, earth-based stargazers' curious observation of the heavens has never waned so much as it has in this recent time frame—specifically from the turning of the millennium, and, even more prevalently, in these few brief years since the ending of the Mayan calendar: December 21, 2012.

You have entered the fast lane of unbridled technological prowess. It has sent your civilization careening in the direction of one that is steadily, willfully turning itself over—from one of conscious, feeling human beings, to robotically manipulated biocomputers of unparalleled, programmed intelligence.

You accept that technology is striving for total takeover of your society—but, somehow, you are certain that you will not let it happen to you—or your children. However, if you are really true with yourselves, you can only admit that electronics has taken a dominant place in your lives, and even more so in those of your young, and that its grip is tightening, affecting almost every aspect of your day-to-day experience. It has so imposed itself upon your creativity and artistry that it is rendering obsolete the acquired and innate human talents for music, art, language, and discovery on every level—just as it is subverting your mental superiority—the acquisition of knowledge through learning and life experience—to the punching of keys.

Computers may not be able to express love, but they **are** the delivery system of pornography, distorting people's perception of love and intimacy, and rendering it in such ways that the magic of love is degraded to a violent or extreme performance of any given sexual act. Such portrayal can only numb the viewer to the experience of true passion: that euphoric feeling one shares when a chemical interaction, body to body, heart to heart, is shared with another human being.

We, who are no longer in physical form, cannot imagine why any corporeal being would prefer such artificial and impersonal stimulation, through a one-dimensional viewing screen, to the touch, the scent, and the warmth of another.

Technology certainly is altering the way you relate to the stars, and how you feel and relate to the movements of celestial transits overhead.

We are not suggesting that your modern-day knowledge of the galactic field is somehow more limited because of your technology: that would be shortsighted, if not completely nonsensical. What we do wish to emphasize, instead, is how the probing of military astro-science, disguised as astronomy, has thrust its way to the stars, to places that are still beyond your knowledge, for reasons that they feel you are not ready to know, nor entitled to access. They provide you with a fraction of what they have captured in digital imaging, and they tell you even less of what they know about the big picture, playing across their cosmic viewing screens. So, be aware. Take no photographic image or digital impression as absolute proof of any truth. Pictures can be digitally altered. Hence, they can never effectively qualify as proof of anything, if "absolute proof" can ever even exist. Utilize them wisely; remember that they are persuasive tools that can be accurate, or altered to create a desired representation of reality.

We hold the fascination of one pondering the heavens on a summer's night up to that of an organization intent upon penetrating or invading space, and invite you to consider how best to establish a balance between the two methods of observation: experience versus information.

Let us not forget that even what you see with your eyes is subject to the filters of the three-dimensional construct, and the space-time conundrum of spatial relationships, which affects and distorts perception. Therein lies the question of time, and whether what stars you are seeing directly, or through sophisticated electronics, actually still exist in the canopy overhead. Are they really there? It may very well be that so many thousands, even millions, of light years from you, a star that holds your fascination, because its light has finally reached you, has, in the meantime, moved on, to another dimension.

In *The Cosmos of Soul,* Book One of our earlier works, we presented you with this question, and we asked you to ponder the illusory aspect of the time it takes starlight to reach you. It is a sound basis from which you can grasp the questions that we raise regarding the illusions of three-dimensional reality. Allow us to refer to a brief quote from that missive:

> *The brightest stars in your night skies*
> *are so many millions of miles from Earth*
> *that it takes years for their light to reach you . . .*

Doesn't that boggle your minds? Surely, when you peer out into the starry canopy of your night skies, you do not consider the possibility that you are actually observing stars and planet bodies as they existed many years ago. So then, on the basis of that hypothesis, it stands to reason that as you look upon the heavens, you are gazing at many stars, millions of miles from Earth, that may actually no longer exist in physical reality. In the process of their evolution, they may have already burned out, exploded, or passed through their own astral cords in the death-rebirth passage. We are suggesting that when you gaze into the heavens it is as if you are looking through a time machine. What you see shining into your eyes and the astronomers' sophisticated telescopes is the light of stars, remote galaxies, and the reflection of heavenly bodies as they existed hundreds, thousands . . . millions of years ago.

> —*The Cosmos of Soul: A Wake-Up Call for Humanity,*
> Book One of the Sirian Revelations Trilogy (Berkeley,
> CA: North Atlantic Books, 2008).

As space exploration still remains off-limits to almost all but those funded governmental agencies that have the technology to achieve it, you are wise to understand that what information is made available to you is always processed through their screens before you are given access. Your own filters—the gut response, your open heart, and your keen intellect—are far more effective resources when it comes to discerning truth. Do remember that discoveries that come from your space agencies are only renditions of reality—designed to conform to what they want you to know and understand, and insofar as they comply with the master plan that regards disclosure of life beyond your boundaries.

The secret government still holds a monopoly on the divulgence of exoplanetary life and communications, and, judging how misrepresentative they are with regards to your own earthly affairs, you can pretty much safely assume that they are even more manipulative where you have no means of weighing their information against any other source that might contradict them.

Support your amateur astronomers! And always remember that the three-dimensional perspective is flawed, as demonstrated by the fact that you cannot even be certain that what you are looking at, up there in the heavens, is actually there. While that may confuse you on the one hand, it gives you solid ground from which to seek your own higher understanding of the makings of reality: that of the third dimension, which is still your framework, and the many other levels or layers of the cosmic truth.

Utilizing discretion over what the secret government wants you to believe, and listening to what you are told with due circumspection, you will be more effective when you access any and all information its agencies provide. Again, at the point of becoming redundant, we invite you always to consider that our perceptions, as six-dimensional beings, and the truth we derive from them, may not correspond with yours, and, therefore, do use that same innate ability to feel what is right for you. Bear in mind that we can provide thoughts and hypotheses that may or may not resonate with you, but we cannot manipulate images and information that purport to be scientifically sound, or representative of factually grounded information, regarding any given situation to which you still cling . . . despite knowing that it has been shown to be illusory in nature!

As for the stars, consider that, as individuals, at that very personal level of experience that your antecedents once accessed in their exploration of the mystical Cosmos, you have all but turned over your love of the heavens to your own electronic distractions, and to those agencies (arms of the corporate/government system that created your personal mind-numbing electronic gadgetry) that explore space on "your behalf."

What have you, as individuals, and as the collective consciousness of Earth, gained from its proliferation, and what have you lost?

When we make reference to "individuals" in this context, we are talking about nearly eight billion people who inhabit the entire expanse of your civilized world. Not everyone is awake, nor paying any attention at all to what is swirling above them, in the celestial canopy . . . not even around them: in the tall grass, blowing through the trees, or washing over crystalline sands. Were it not for the starseed, astrologers, pagan worshippers, natives, and astronomers amongst you, who would be observing the movements and energies of the celestial deities above? Anyone?

Most human beings inhabiting Earth at this time do not seem to need the stars anymore, or to recognize planets on distant horizons. Locked inside four walls, they seem to have forsaken the magic of heavenly visions, which elude now—more than ever before—yielding to "content" provided on the viewing screen.

The great philosophers have gone, their wisdom usurped by sterile information, and an unfathomable proliferation of data. When comes another Aristotle, orating from the great Parthenon, where he and his enthralled students sat, in the warm hours of Grecian night, contemplating the godliness of stars and the movements of illuminated planets? The master, Pythagoras of Samos, connected all the dots, from star to star, and all that existed in between, in geometric synchronicities. What of him, and the cosmic wisdom he brought to your world?

They, and other star worshippers like them, belonged to another era, one of many that coalesced with the great spirit of civilizations around the globe: ancient Africa and its Egypt, Atlantis, Mesopotamia, India, China, and those of all the native tribes of the unspoiled Earth.

Farmers, at least those of your industrialized societies, no longer consider the waxing or waning of the moon. They have lost touch with the natural biology of their process, and the effect the moon's gravitational swings hold over seed that will lie in the earth, awaiting the cosmically attuned time for optimum propagation.

Genetically modified seeds have been desensitized from receiving such cosmic signals; and farmers, in turn, have lost the sensitivity to note the difference.

Machines and chemicals push mass production to its limits now, and the sun and the moon are secondary considerations to those mechanizations. As a result, and because of this disregard for the subtle forces of nature—forces perpetually altered and progressively dominated by man— crops derived from your twenty-first-century agriculture industry are increasingly devoid of their vitality and essence. They no longer sustain and promote healthy life: not as they did before—neither their own, nor yours. And they are increasingly harmful, toxic, and disruptive to all body systems—including those of the animal and insect communities, who also feed of their bounty.

Modern-day sailors have lost their need and, hence, their fascination for the stars, for they are fully equipped with navigation systems that have rendered constellations and stellar clusters unnecessary. Satellite tracking systems manage all of that now . . . not man, whose sense of direction and course through the open oceans depended upon the light and position of the stars.

Urban blight, city lights, and those undeniable chemical trails that grid your lower atmosphere with toxic residue—so dense you no longer see your own sun for days on end—have dramatically dimmed, and in places, they have totally obliterated, the star-filled night sky. How can you be drawn to contemplate the greater universe, if the light of billions of stars is lost to you, by neon signs and highways of electric illuminations?

But then again, are you even looking? Have you noticed the sky has all but gone out over your most heavily populated urban centers? Who, of you, can say, without hesitation, that you still take that precious time to gaze in wonder of the heavens, especially on those nights when clear skies bedazzle with the diamond lights of so many stars?

No doubt your contemporary society's disassociation from the designs and activities that permeate and penetrate your night skies stems not only from the array of computerized distractions made available to you all, but also from a drastically reduced visual field from the one your ancestors enjoyed. It was not so very long ago, when the Earth was free of pollutants, when your skies were not obliterated by those geoengineered clouds, and when the proliferation of electric lights in your urban and suburban centers made it almost impossible to see any other night lights, but those of your own creation.

Keeping you locked away in your houses, a growing fear of violence and danger pervades the night hours, where once you felt free to lie on a sandy beach and pass the night looking up: wondering, dreaming. Then, too, there is a sharp increase in disturbed atmospheric conditions, with their raging weather systems, that keep you indoors.

One cannot overlook the immense pressures that you face, just to survive and maintain your contemporary lifestyles. You work so hard to provide for yourself and your families, whose needs and demands from a consumption society often exceed your capabilities. Some of you, closed in cement buildings and cubicles, during those long hours of your working days, barely see the light at all.

Who has time to stargaze?

By the time you return home, your bodies and minds are so fatigued that they crave mindless distractions to unplug from the daily race. Ironically, that is anything but a disconnect, for it entrains you even more, through the mind-numbing network that provides television, computer games, and all the other holograms that take you from presence—the now of experience—to the "What's on?" mentality, glued to your screen of preference.

And so, unlike your antecedents, you are spending far more stargazing hours behind four walls, indoors—disengaged from everything around you. The light of billions of stars, the regular movements of the planets, the sway of the moon, and regular appearances of extraterrestrial ships—even your own spacecraft—go pretty much ignored, in favor of whatever programming is being served up, on any given night, for mass consumption.

What possibly could go wrong?

And yet, paradoxically, everything about your position in the galaxy of matter, and, more precisely, as the primary communication station orbiting your sun, Ra, is at its most enticing. Your cosmic environment is buzzing, to say the least! There is a cosmic dance of evolving planets; the sun is in complete metamorphosis; Earth's poles are tilting, shifting the positions of the sun and moon on the horizon. Not to mention, of course, the proliferation of alien visitors and observation teams, and their light probes of all dimensions and formations, moving across the skies—night and day.

Are you paying attention?

Some of you have never even bothered to look up.

Others look, but see nothing, wondering: where have the stars gone?

Since the earliest days of Atlantis, we speak of one hundred thousand years ago, human consciousness has been flooded with a vast assortment of hypotheses, beliefs, and opinions regarding the nature of the Cosmos. These notions of man's place in the greater sphere of existence were often formed not only from mythology and science, but also from actual interaction with alien visitors: scientists, engineers, aviators, and biologists from several other domains in the physical universe.

You have only to observe ancient carvings, designs in the landscapes, and hieroglyphs in deep, prehistoric caves, to know the truth of alien interaction with Earth, at many points in history, to be undeniable—although many deny it still. Prehistoric drawings of beings in space gear (bearing uncanny resemblance to your present-day astronauts), staring back at you from temples and landscapes around the world, cannot be ignored.

Surely conventional archeology dismisses it.

Why the global society of the Earth allows that deception to continue has everything to do with the illusory nature of your dimension—and how you can see with your physical eyes, although they do not necessarily cut through the appearance of truth to get to its core . . . its essence. That is all the more relevant to you since the last twenty years (or even earlier, with the advent of television), when the technology industry decided for you what was truth, so that you wouldn't have to search for it any further!

Through this system overall, and every single time you tune in to it—be aware: you are allowing someone to implant a false or skewed understanding of reality through the designs of their creation, and of truth, as they desire to depict it.

That will change, and for some of you it has already, when you see clearly through your extrasensory multidimensional experience, and shut down the holographic network.

Science, academia, and the establishment's positioned "authorities" on the nature of the Cosmos have pulled contemporary earth civilization, or shall we say the "developed" world, away from belief in celestial gods, and explained away the forces of the universe in chemical, mechanical, and technical terms. They have attempted to cast off any other belief or perception that defies scientific terms, even if those terms are often based on erroneous theory and limited "laws."

We are not intent upon negating the great benefits and significant leaps gleaned from the scientific persuasions. Nor do we deny how scientific observation has expanded your understanding of certain aspects of reality and the universe at large, even if it still grapples with the very concept of Creation, insofar as astrophysicists will not rest until they can somehow finally define the "beginning" of the universe.

The problem, you see, is that once again, they are using outdated laws of physics, physics that apply to the Earth, to try to describe a macrocosm of which they still know so very little.

We ask you to consider this: if you were back in the time of the Great Inquisition, presenting your big bang theories, you would be almost instantly condemned to a torturous death for your heretical ideas: science. Many great thinkers were. Spirit didn't fare much better back then—and only strict obedience to the dominating religion would have spared you from being chastised, banned, or burned for your belief in any representation other than that of the religious hierarchy and its portrayal of Prime Creator—God—and the fervent adherence to the rules of the established church.

Even today, daring "New Age" teachers, alternative healing proponents, and unorthodox spiritualists are met with ridicule, offense, threats, and even elimination. It is still dangerous to challenge the system, especially when your truth blatantly exposes its deceptions, lies, and treachery.

Is it any wonder that science and spirit have struggled to find one unified field that leads back to the stars?

The idea of a "big bang" in the cosmic halls of Creation, which triggered everything that exists, is so antithetical to anything that resembles the laws of creative design. Despite all the empirical knowledge gleaned from these sources, we are suggesting that the perception of celestial and universal experience, described by earlier civilizations through myth and mystical interpretations of the forces of nature on Earth and beyond, was often far closer to the truth of the nature of all reality than your scientists understand it to be today.

True, your technological progression, over the last two hundred years, has been staggering. You have become so advanced that you are capable of direct observation of space via satellites, probes, space travel, and through significant breakthroughs in your understanding of quantum mechanics and physics. You have extraterrestrial advisors working with your governments, providing extreme technology that is propelling you away from your humanity, toward a robotic society. Some of these beings are so similar to you in form that you would not even notice them if they stood before you. Others, such as the archetypal Greys and the less familiar Insectoids,[10] have colonized the substrata, coming and going, at will, in military and governmental structures there, as is necessary for the perpetration of their mutual agendas with those who direct your political leaders.

On the other hand, there have always been highly gifted psychics who can shift dimensions, time travel, and provide prophetic perspectives on the future. You also have exoplanetary physical beings, from outside your solar system, but also from within, who are active members of the galactic fraternity of peaceful civilizations, helping you to avoid total destruction of your civilization, and all life that comprises its rich biodiversity.

Multidimensional councils, such as ours, serve as guides and counsel for the spiritual progression of life in the earth realm. Gaia, herself, teaches you that no destruction is irreparable, no wound permanent. All things eventually heal and are rebirthed. All of these contribute to what is served

---

[10]   http://aliens.wikia.com/wiki/Insectoid

up to you at this time of accelerated awareness of, or at the very least, curiosity about, what lies beyond.

The polarity, the swing back and forth between darkness and light, the future . . . the past, everything is directing you toward resolution.

All is written in the stars.

5

Cosmic Soup

It is so utterly impossible to imagine an infinite physical universe, with its trillions of stars, and billions of galaxies—especially when you have stopped looking with your own eyes! To then ponder the possibility that each of these could exist, in parallel universes, is almost too much for the mind to even consider, much less comprehend.

Filled with perpetual crisis on personal and societal levels, the average individual has little time or desire to consider the bigger picture: why the Cosmos? What is its purpose? How immense could it possibly be? Does it have confines, boundaries?

And what of the space-time continuum?

It is, in so many ways, much easier to leave these contemplations to the scientists, and they are more than happy that you do just that: leave the Cosmos to them; entrust space exploration and extraplanetary life to the "experts."

We cannot emphasize enough how very masterfully the elite, who still rule over you, have gotten you to focus your awareness upon the distractions of daily life. Their orchestrations keep you particularly spellbound by events, surroundings, and illusions that activate you in the lower energies of fear, survival, and desire—and keep you bound to the emotions that are stirred in those powerful electromagnetic energy wheels of your bodies: the chakras.

The irony of "progress" is that it inevitably distracts people from the greater picture of their place in the grand cosmic theater, and focuses them upon the minutiae that constitute living, day to day, and all that is entailed in maintaining a comfortable physical existence: consuming more than is needed, striving to obtain more . . . and by and large, allowing the desire inherent in both to perpetuate the impossibility of ever being satisfied, grateful, and satiated.

The consumption system, put in place by the corporate overlords, thrives on your dissatisfaction, so do not look for resolution outside of yourself. It is a simple fact that the less you feel you need, the happier you will be with your life—which, in turn, stimulates the contemplation of the higher purpose and deeper meaning of existence: all existence, not just your own. They do not want that. You are not supposed to aspire to higher aspects of your individual experience, for the ripples that they send into the collective consciousness are an absolutely unwelcome contribution to those who are busy controlling it, where they are using every method imaginable to manipulate your desire, through the lower frequencies of the human spirit.

If you are ruled by the events of your daily lives, struggling to keep yourselves afloat, you will not be interested in the deeper, existential questions that take you to loftier places in your mind, and then to greater aspirations for society at large. If you are struggling to stay afloat financially, conflicted about your sexual identity, or allowing yourself to be used as a punching bag in the perennial fight of opposing religions, politicians, educators, physicians, and all the other programmers of social behavior, you will be too distracted to be asking questions about the true nature of the Cosmos, over which the secret government prefers to maintain as much control as possible . . . and to restrict the pace of human awakening.

If you understand that what governmental agencies feed the public is not at all the cutting edge of their existing knowledge or recent discoveries, and certainly not Truth, you will be more capable of seeing through their smokescreens. You will be more trusting of your own free thought impressions, because your own curiosity and wonder spark your DNA highways, where all information is stored. That, in turn, sends light racing through your molecular fabric, through the blood and organs, and the neural networks. That is the bioelectromagnetic activity that describes illumination, in every sense.

The system doles out bits and pieces of information that their secret technology has already rendered old and outdated, leaving you, seekers, to find your own way upon the galactic speedway that is racing you to your next destination. Ironically, in ways they never anticipated and have yet to understand, it has empowered you to overcome the repression of knowledge, and it has weakened its control over you—simply by squeezing you too hard, for too long.

We understand how taxing it can be for you, intellectually, to try to fathom interacting dimensions, or densities of consciousness, that have no beginnings or endings, or how they co-exist, perpetually, being birthed and passing away to other states of reality. Just as all biological beings enjoy the spring and winter of their days, so do all conscious aspects of the universe experience their birth into the physical, acquiring what they need to grow and to fully experience their life cycle. And when that is complete, they pass from one world to another, or one dimension to the next, continuing their infinite progression of consciousness, and then returning, to Source.

This is the soul essence of the Cosmos, the perfect design of Creation— being constantly birthed, flourishing, interacting, fading, contributing to the collective consciousness, and eventually passing to another density, realm, or lifetime.

More spiritually developed societies of your current and ancient worlds have always understood that there is no beginning, and no end, to the Cosmos of Soul. The gift that emerges from that awareness extends to your personal lives, inviting the existential consideration: that you are immortal, eternal and infinite consciousness, transmuting form, perpetually evolving, playing divine music across the strings of forever. It helps you to understand that what goes on, in what seems to be the unknowable multiverse, is simply a reflection of your own form, energy patterns, and conscious creation.

No amount of scientific data will ever be available that can quantify or explain the celestial dynamics of the physical, three-dimensional universe, much less the complexities of higher dimensions, for there is no spirit in deductive reasoning. It is cold and calculating, and it lacks soul and the spirit of wonder. How then could it possibly explore the soul of Creation? Without a sense of wonder, how can one possibly contemplate the remarkable proliferation of life, in all its beauty and diversity, in an exquisitely designed, interactive universe?

The light of countless stars pierces the darkness, all the nights of your days. Some are long gone, but their light has still not gone out in your quadrant of space. Planets dance and whirl, and align, at times, in specific cosmometric designs, showing themselves to you in precise formations.

There are markers, indicators of some organization to the spectrum of structures and great celestial beings that form the tapestry of the universe. It is still a visual field from which you can glean a sense of the infinite, as did your ancestors, but it is nothing compared to what you are about to experience accessing the fourth dimension.

If you think the physical universe is complex, brace yourself for how the multiverse is opening up to you: intricate and mysterious. Here is where unbridled spirit soars past science, theory, and mechanics—where you experience so many more layers of the divine consciousness woven into the tapestry of the Cosmos. It will be the light of Spirit that guides that exploration, and you will need no satellites, rockets, and craft to break through all the barriers that have never been barriers at all—at least not as we perceive and intend them.

We, too, are travelers through that which we wish to depict as an infinite cosmic soup, and we will stretch and remold this metaphor, as best we can, to bring to you our understanding of dimensions, timelessness, and the interrelationship between physicality and refined states of consciousness. If you will push your imagination to allow for some incongruities between metaphor and reality, we will take you through a highly oversimplified process that we hope can be grasped more simply than quantum mechanics and higher physics could dare attempt.

The question of who prepares the soup or, better yet, contemplation of who even thought of it, to begin with, we prefer to leave to your own interpretation of who, or what, constitutes Prime Creator. That is so personal to all souls, throughout Creation, and no one individual, nor religion, nor belief system can ever truly prove its existence: neither to the self, nor to anyone else. You are wise and empowered when you let no one impose that upon you, for no one, across the greater expanse of the Cosmos, can ever tell another what, or who, that is. In fact, let us reemphasize that anyone, or any system, that dares demand your allegiance to its "core values" or tenets, or one that requires blind allegiance and obedience, is not aligned with the idea that we are all sovereign beings, on our sacred paths—one, and all—to find our way to the Essence.

You do know there is a divine code laced throughout life—you need not search far to find it: it is in human DNA, just as it is found in the molecular structure of an ant, or the fibers in a leaf. We shall never attempt to convince you, whatsoever, how it got there or who designed it, for, as we just said, we all have a very personal understanding of gods and creators, and we honor each individual's freedom to believe, or not to believe, in anything . . . anything at all.

No doubt there are those of you, reading these words, who do not believe in any god or primal force, preferring not to give time to its contemplation. However, for the sake of this discourse, we invite you to understand that, in our experience and understanding (which need not be yours), there exists a Prime Creator—the Great Master Chef of Creation, who pooled together all the ingredients of the All That Is, That Ever Was, and That Always Will Be to cook up the brew of the Cosmos, just as our allegorical chef will do—in this, our treatise on a metaphorical pot of vegetable soup.

For the sake of our focus here, we begin this dissertation observing that, despite its liquidity, vegetable soup does contain bits of relatively dense matter. There are larger pieces of vegetables; there are smaller elements, such as spices, herbs, and other seasonings. And of course, the less dense and pervading element, water, the base of its existence, serves to blend all the other elements together, in a unifying field into which all other aspects are incorporated, transmuting, from their individual character, to merge with other elements.

Each of these has its purpose, in relationship to the quality of the soup: its density, its flavor, color, scent, etc. Each is individual, with its own properties, and yet, in the context of this soup, it is merely an aspect that contributes to the whole.

You may wonder what in the world we are speaking of here, and how it is relevant to a discussion of Creation.

Stay with us.

This broth, with its bits and pieces, carries and reflects consciousness throughout its constitution. Above all, it is the manifestation of its creator, the chef, who unites elements (s)he understands will create a perfect soup. It contains the chef's intention, the wisdom and the understanding of what works in the making of it, for without that intention, any cook's creation can be an utter disaster. The mere setting out to create something wonderful laces it with that love and focused mind.

Everything within it—from the water to the smallest elements, even salt crystals—reflects awareness, for all is comprised of DNA, the divine architecture of all things inherent in all Creation. They are structures that are formed of chemical elements, subatomic particles, and atoms . . . but more importantly, they are units of consciousness that contain mathematically precise codes: the god code.

There are aspects to this vegetable soup that have a more solid quality to their consistency, where the vegetable particles are still intact, or beginning to break down from the cooking process, and others where the watery essence that binds everything together is still relatively clear, more like a broth, and therefore more expansive in consistency.

An energetic force provides the heat to cook this brew. To the chef, it is the flame, or the electric coil—both expressions of directed energy. Remembering whatever you have learned in the kitchens of your own experience, or in basic chemistry classes in school, you know that heat expands; cold constricts. This is how the matrix of the physical universe is manipulated—we will describe it in short order, but let us not digress here.

Now, let us imagine the steam formed from the cooking of this matrix. It seems to be separate from the actual soup, but it is not. It is a less dense representation of those ingredients, or that process; it is of a different quality than, but of the same essence as, the soup itself.

Think about this. Isn't that steam as much a part of the soup, and of the process that led to its creation, as it is of its outcome? Doesn't it carry the soup's scent throughout the space in which it has simmered, affecting the space around it? If you have observed how a window becomes opaque from the steam of such a cooking process, you know that, theoretically, you cannot separate the phenomenon of steam from the brew. It is of a different form and consistency, a less dense aspect of the soup, but still it is the soup . . . and that, sweet souls, is an overly simplified depiction of the higher dimensions, in relationship to the universe of matter.

Consider the philosophical issue here: within the steam that permeates the kitchen, and fogs the walls and windows, is contained the consciousness of the soup itself, described above. It contains a more refined form of the chef's creative intent, and the conscious nature of all the elements used to create the brew.

If you ask us to define "ascension" in a few simple words, we would be comfortable using this depiction: it is an immensely bigger version of the transformative evolution from soup to steam, from steam to vapor, from vapor to pure energy, conscious memory, etheric scent. Should the glue that has bound it there yield to the humidity of that vapor, even wallpaper that bubbles or peels away would contain the cellular memory of that experience.

You do see that even in a structured context, such as the third dimension, there is no way to define these aspects as separate from each other, other than to consider manifestation, essence, and density as reflections of the original conscious intent of the chef, the soup's creator.

Let us now compare our microcosmic pot of vegetable soup—all that it contains . . . and in all its manifestations—to the infinite cosmic soup—the chemical elements and subatomic particles of the material universe that comprise its ingredients.

Here there is no pot for the chef. It is electromagnetism that is the glue that binds it all together.

Yet, its essence is so similar, is it not? It is comprised of very dense matter, such as crafts, satellites, extreme minerals, all sorts of celestial spheres, rocks, and less dense elements, such as biological elements, ice, dust, chemicals, fire, gas, and water. All are ingredients of the pervasive cosmic substance, and, as you understand, all contain consciousness.

If you are still reticent to declare a rock "conscious," read back to the introduction of this book, to reexamine the fossil imbedded in a mineral matrix. Then again, minerals contain highly complex geometries and mathematical proportions, right down to their molecular structure. And what of the crystal kingdom? You cannot disagree that certain minerals, quartz in particular, retain memory, expand upon it, and reflect it back into the ethers. If that is a consideration too metaphysical for your tastes, remind yourself that silicon is crystal—and that computer technology, throughout every aspect of its immense application, is dependent upon quartz crystal, for reasons we have just described.

Whether Prime Creator created the cosmic soup to nourish, to entertain, or to simply express him/her/itself—you have to admit that nothing, no possible contemplation of the heavens, no intellectual discourse, and no hypothesis can possibly outshine the wonder of **why.**

Why does the universe exist at all? That quintessential question may never find resolution, so vast are the possibilities of its creation . . . in all their interpretations. Perhaps it is never meant to be known, but, rather, to be held to the light of our inquisitive minds, compelling us to make something quite spectacular of our lives.

Without wonder, how dull would be the journey.

Without stars, how dim the light.

Inspiration is found in the seeking, not the knowing, for once we have acquired understanding of anything, we set out on a higher quest, carrying that awareness to our next destination, or the next puzzle. And oh, what a field of possibilities exists from which we can glean the inspiration and the wisdom: from the formation of the cosmic soup, to the infinity of the Cosmos of Soul.

That wonder—the wonder of it all—is truly our way home: to that hearth within us all, and to the flame of all Creation—the source of all light.

6

Navigating the Fourth Dimension

While you stand in anticipation of this great stellar metamorphosis, and as a reflection of the accelerating energies that surround and permeate your star, you may already recognize that you, yourselves, are already intermittently interacting with the fourth dimension. So is your sun; so are all things within its entirety, all the way to the farthest reaches, and past all planets you know... and others that you have yet to discover.

Like some cosmic litmus paper, fluttering on a gentle breeze, it is the outer edge of the fourth density that overlaps with areas of your solar system, as it tests the sun's alchemical preparedness for transitioning to a far more refined electromagnetic and conscious expanse.

That solar energy is ready to rise—to race, in its entirety, through its astral cord, like a great kundalini explosion that detonates its physical light through galactic space, ejects its material skin, and soars, refined and released from the constraints of matter and form, into the vibratory field of its next great existential adventure.

We know that you can visualize this, in the mind's eye, for you do understand how energy works. You do know this; it is coded into every cell of your being. You can grasp the enormity of just such a solar phenomenon if you remember that it happens on so many smaller, more manageable levels, in the same way: energy rising, exploding, and changing form. What is most likely difficult for you to envision, instead, is how possibly you can be jetted through this process unfazed, and still retain "I am" awareness . . . or just how the new vibrational environment will still resemble and reflect the world you left behind, in the "outer skin" of your metamorphic passage.

You, and every living being, throughout your solar system, are going along for this ride, and that is a destiny of stellar proportions! And, in the case of those starseed amongst you, who found your way to Planet Earth to serve in the transition, it is a karmic reward: for your sacrifice, your service, and the wisdom you have brought from star systems far and near.

You may already realize that your personal and individual experience of the fourth may be brief—a mere stopover for karmic cleansing, if it is your soul destiny to leap into still higher realms.

Let that not concern you.

It is the ego that yearns to know about levels of attainment, not the soul. In the cosmic scheme of things, it is unimportant. Indeed, true achievement of all spiritual and emotional progression is found in appreciation of the now, through the love of all that is present, and in gratitude for all that **is.**

Let the ego be calmed in the light of unknowable wonder. Be in that "now" of your experience; find the beauty in that state of being. Feel the subtlety—don't miss the nuances, for they are the greatest gifts life offers. Let the electric, empirical mind be cooled in the magnetism of your reflective pool—the intuitive center—where all wisdom is held, and from whence you have access to everything you need to navigate the dimensions.

Although we do not deny that there will be aspects of the fourth dimension that are going to challenge your credulity in very substantial ways, especially in the preliminary experience, blinking in and out of it, as you have begun to do—we assure you that it is going to be a glorious ride.

Bearing in mind our earlier considerations of the unreliability of digital imaging, we observe that this grandiose display of matter, transmuting to a more refined energetic frequency, is readily available to you, through solar imaging (provided by the Solar and Heliospheric Observatory, the SOHO[11] project). It provides you with select images of your sun, engaging in a partial disappearing and reappearing act. Participating government-funded scientists, engineers, and astrophysicists confess to having little or no understanding of just what is occurring in that plasma vortex, which could explain the appearance and disappearance of coronal holes in the center of the sun.

They are, admittedly, "baffled."

A recurring theme now, scientists' "bafflement" over everything that does not fit the mold, the law, or the precept, seems to be occurring across

---

[11] https://sohowww.nascom.nasa.gov

the field of their investigations with greater regularity, the more information they acquire.

However, we can tell you that those immense licks of plasma have begun shooting into the fourth dimension, and then merging back into the three-dimensional solar form, its plasma body, within the dynamic that you know as the star's gaseous "structure."

We trust you will agree that this extraordinary metamorphosis, captured regularly now in the photographic record, can be considered "real," relative to your three-dimensional experience, even if those same astrophysicists and scientists remain irreconcilably perplexed by the phenomenon.

With respect for these individuals, some of whom are dedicated researchers, we note that they cannot access or perceive multidimensionality, because it is not available to the reasoning, mathematical mind. Let us reiterate here, for the sake of emphasizing a point, in your own awareness, that you may have reached long ago. That is, that anything to do with the interface of dimensions is of such a subtle nature, it may be imperceptible to those who are still bound to the process of data acquisition, empirical thinking, and the gathering of information from anything outside of personal experience. Unfathomable to them, in terms of their understanding of the laws they believe govern the universe, it remains a scientific conundrum.

No wonder quantum physics is moving into the foreground, for it represents the emergence of human consciousness, at a time when new laws must be found to describe unfolding cosmic events that are being perceived by your current generations as reality. Quantum physics provides a pathway to the merging of two conscious approaches to understanding what actually happens during stellar ascension, and to the planetary bodies, in kind. It opens you to understanding your own, individual ascension process, the likes of which no one, in your immediate realm, has yet experienced—at least, not in the present lifetime—and one that only limited numbers of you can truly fathom deeply, personally, and with great anticipation, rather than in dread and fear.

The truth is that it is not necessary that you understand this intellectually to experience it viscerally. In fact, in so many ways, the intellectual brain that gathers knowledge and processes data is a constant hindrance, for it perpetually attempts to override the intuitive mind. It craves dominion over the aspect of your consciousness that is capable of perceiving subtle phenomena and otherworldly events; it aims to rationalize away any idea of other dimensions, parallel realities, and any other framework that does not fit into the mold of 3D perception.

In essence, that part of your brain, the data processor, seeks linear solutions to a completely nonlinear environment.

You can understand the conflict between the two hemispheres of your brain as the same divide between scientific and spiritual approaches to the questions of universal transition. How odd, though, that the logical mind can be overridden by holographic computer games, where the generated imaging redirects the hardwiring of the brain to behave and to perceive itself within artificial constructs! Do you understand the implications of such interference in your natural brain waves?

Nonetheless, we do hear your call for further clarity, and we are prepared to provide what we can, to help you take that leap of faith, and awareness, that will help you adjust to the phenomena of dimension shift—actively occurring now, in different degrees of intensity and velocity. Your task is to hold a balance between the left and right hemispheres of your brain—of knowledge and wisdom—which will be immensely important to your ability to integrate those aspects into a cohesive view of the multiverse.

Like you, your central sun, the planetary and moon-like formations that orbit it, and all biological beings that live within and upon them, are blinking in and out of the fourth density—still pretty much unsure of what is happening, or how it is manifesting, and even less aware of the "when" or "why" of it. Know that these sporadic and seemingly inexplicable events will become more frequent in the time ahead of you, which we cannot specifically measure in terms that will satisfy your curiosity, because, when it comes to multidimensionality, there are no fixed measures.

To attempt to give you a determined time line for the no-time is, at best, what you would call an "oxymoron" of the highest order!

However, we are very comfortable in declaring, unequivocally, that, although life in your solar system is still anchored in the illusory dynamics of the third dimension, all beings, even the self-aware celestial bodies that bear such life, are now occasionally experiencing themselves in the no-time of the fourth dimension. Its duration can be just a second . . . a flash, and then gone, barely comprehensible. Or it can last long enough for you to recognize that you are on unfamiliar ground: warped time, heightened awareness, telepathic communication, and a sense of momentary displacement. That has begun to happen, in varying degrees, and it will be accelerating in the days, months, and years ahead.

Consider the primary milestones in this progressive phase of your elusive, but nonetheless decisive, evolutionary framework, and note that you surely resonate with a few simple guidelines. We trust they will show how you are already experiencing that:

* Time is no longer a constant that you can depend on.

* The animals are behaving erratically or disappearing altogether. They are also slipping ahead of you, into the fourth dimension. Not all species extinction occurrences are due to imbalance of the ecosystems, or the human hand.

* You are becoming more perceptive, beyond the framework of the physical senses, experiencing activation of the pineal gland.

* The earth, your ground, is shifting everywhere around you: volcanoes, quakes, sinkholes, the crumbling mantle. It is as if Gaia herself is showing you how what you consider "solid" is anything but that.

* All things of a structural nature, including the hierarchy that has built its power of domination over you, are crumbling. Nothing can hold; only fluidity of spirit and place is the constant, and the security.

Overall, as you are beginning to experience the outer edges of the fourth dimension, your awareness of it is still limited to very brief moments, in which glitches in the space-time continuum occur. Significant mutations and their unfamiliar manifestations of time either warping, or disappearing completely, will have you off-balance while you are in the experience, and before you come back fully to three-dimensional awareness. These brief flickers will increase in frequency and duration, experienced as alterations in time. They are similar to the "déjà vu" experience, through which you relive something you believe already happened in the past . . . or in its opposite manifestation—leaping into the future, an experience that you will find best described through our channel's own words. Having assisted her through the warp, we ask her to share, with you, her experience of just such a blinking into the fourth dimension and back into 3D.

It was the summer of 2016—I had just immigrated to an island in the middle of the Atlantic. My house was under massive reconstruction, so I had to rent a place to stay until the work was completed and I could finally move back in.

Situated on this rental property was the main house where I was staying, and a separate cottage, which the owner rented out on Airbnb. During my stay, I experienced significant movement of holiday renters, checking in and out, and frequent encounters with the owner, who came and went almost every other day, preparing the cottage for each new guest.

One afternoon, at precisely 5:00 P.M., I heard a car pull up into the driveway, and park next to the cottage entrance. I couldn't avoid hearing the loud, travel-weary voices of a man and woman, speaking in Italian, with a very distinct Venetian accent, which I recognized, having spent half my life in Italy. As they unloaded the car, its doors opening and slamming shut, a baby started screaming at the top of its lungs, and it was obvious, from the sound of things, that they were new arrivals. I remember thinking to myself, "Oh boy, Italians! I'll have to introduce myself in the morning."

The next morning, the owner dropped by. I heard her car arrive, and park where the Italians had parked the night before, but they had apparently gone out early, as their car was gone. I peeked my head out to see her loaded down with sheets, towels, and cleaning products, heading for the cottage, which seemed odd, since her guests were already in. I greeted her and said, "I see you have Italians staying!"

She looked shocked. "How did you know they are Italians?" she replied. "They don't even arrive until tomorrow."

When I insisted that they had indeed come in the night before, and how I had heard them speaking outside, she became agitated and ran up the stairs to the cottage. To my complete amazement, she found no sign of any people having been there. The cottage was empty: no bags, no baby, nothing.

The next day, this precise scene repeated itself. At 5:00 P.M. on the dot, I heard a car pull into the driveway and park. I heard the exact same voices, speaking Italian in a Venetian dialect, a baby screaming at the top of its lungs, these same two exasperated people unpacking the car and finally entering the cottage. I looked out the window this time and saw them there, just entering the place.

This experience left me quite unnerved. It was unlike any other supernatural vision I'd ever had. In this instance, I felt that I had somehow slipped into the future, witnessed the events of the next day, and then come back to 3D. But it wasn't a telepathic experience. It had to be something slipping, outside of my previous experiences—the time lines . . . reality . . . dimensions. I have never been able to put it into any frame or reference point that made sense to me.

Had it not been for the fact that I have experiences walking between the worlds, or even more significantly, that I have been receiving assistance from the Council to prepare me for full emergence into the fourth dimension, I don't know how I would have coped with that experience.

Similar things are occurring frequently now. There is no question in my mind, whatsoever, that time is simply evaporating, and that we are about to experience full immersion into the fourth dimension.

As you consider what transpired, and give thought to Trydjya's understanding of what was an unsettling experience, be aware that it is not going to be necessary to possess heightened psychic capabilities to experience these permutations of time, as your 3D planet interfaces with the fourth dimension. Perhaps her perplexity over this event was based upon her childhood experience, for she has always understood paranormal activity to exhibit certain recognizable qualities and manifestations. But this was quite different. She essentially slipped into the fourth dimension, which so closely resembles the third that it can be indiscernible, and from that framework, she plucked a simultaneous time occurrence from the no-time of that density.

What is noteworthy here is that a highly tuned clairvoyant, such as she, could discern no difference between the third and fourth dimension, until they fell back onto each other, in a manner of speaking. The same occurred in the temple of Abydos, where she and others momentarily experienced this sacred portal in the fourth dimension, and became so disoriented when they came back to the third, with images of and references to the temple that simply were not there. This is a very particular aspect of this transmutation, and again, we remind you that it is going to be very confusing for you, for some time.

It is fascinating to us, as it may be to you, how some individuals, such as Trydjya, have that innate capacity to journey the waves of higher dimensions, as if they were hardwired for it, from their birth into the physical realm. Many of you bring these abilities through the birth canal and have somehow managed, throughout your earthly lifetimes, to experience the dance of the multiverse, as it flows to the rhythm of the Cosmic Soul. There are others, as well, who have developed these skills through rigorous spiritual practice, on both sides of the spectrum, for there are also powerful dark magicians where there are brilliant lightworkers, and only intent determines how these abilities manifest.

Even your covert military has developed mind-control programs whereby subjects in training are taught to use a part of their brains to remotely view other realms. They do, in a sense, access the fourth dimension when they apply those skills and the technologies that can help propel them to that density, for brief glimpses of what lies beyond the physical plane. Should you wonder and stress over their visions of what lies ahead, based on those observations, do remember that they are limited to the constraints of their intentions, undoubtedly of the military persuasion. By those limiting channels, they cannot reach beyond that station . . . and they receive and bring back whatever their intention resonates to.

They are not programmed to seek beauty; they are not operating from love.

Love and compassion, those lofty aspects of existence, are the vehicles of souls reaching higher. Only clear consciousness, and the consideration for, respect for, and delight in all Creation, can show any seeker the way into the brilliance.

Sometimes you actually utilize the fourth dimension to pop into a simultaneous physical world where you actually have witnessed yourself in a past or future context; you then pop back into your present reality base where, as we have indicated, you believe is held your core reality—or primary self.

It is confusing to conceptualize that, but it will become easier for you, the more you play upon these time trampolines, with your eyes open, rather than being catapulted through astral acrobatics when you still believe your feet are planted on the ground.

For the whole of society, the occurrence of these phenomena are still the exception, occurring for only brief moments—or, rather, as we have described, for individuals who "blink in and out" of an unfamiliar reality where time is no longer the measure. The distraction factor is far more convincing than a blip in the fabric of time, and the experience may completely escape them. If the mind's lens is focused on video "entertainment," or fixated upon computer-based workstations and smartphones, it cannot be sensitized to the "flickering" between the realms. That would be akin to trying to observe an old-fashioned television apparatus that cannot hold a signal firmly enough to give a clear, steady image.

How do you measure your own missing time and telepathic experiences as being specific to your transition to the fourth dimension, rather than serving as reflections of your own familiar psychic visions? We cannot answer that question for you. We can only illuminate aspects of the process, and indicate signs to watch for. The rest is your journey to experience. All depends upon your readiness, upon your attention to what is happening within and around you and, no less important, upon a very distinct sense of what you came to Earth to witness, and to be part of, at the soul level.

The sooner you understand that this is not a process of human beings alone—and by that we speak not only of intelligent extraterrestrial life forms, but of all those biological expressions that flourish, on all worlds—the sooner you will recognize the effect this shift is having upon everything that exists, around and within you.

It is not merely the more developed species, such as yours, who are evolving to this density. Trees, ocean creatures, even the insect communities are flickering into the fourth dimension and back to the third. Their communal experience of it, together with gross earth changes, are affecting flight patterns, migratory routes, growth cycles, and their behaviors—across the globe, and upon all planetary bodies within your solar field.

What you will retrieve from these early stages of four-dimensional awareness has everything to do with your understanding that you are **not** constrained by 3D, and that you do traverse the waves from the heart, always seeking purification of your own existence. You understand these hypersensory capabilities to be the gifts of karmic achievement in other lifetimes, but they do also represent the soul's purpose in the current lifetime. You may be unaware of it, but you have more of your brain plugged in to more of your rebundling DNA, and the switchboard in the mind connects you (at least momentarily) with manifest consciousness from other dimensions.

We speak to those of you who do enjoy these heightened faculties to remind you that, regardless of how you have acquired them, you are the exception, or at least you have been, until this time when Gaia herself is pulling out of 3D, traversing the outer realms of the fourth dimension.

What is perhaps more significant is that now, aspects of four-dimensional density, particularly regarding the slipping of time, are becoming increasingly evident to even the most unaware—individuals who have no idea, at all, of that which is out of reach of their primal senses.

Like some monumental conveyor belt in the Cosmos, the time lines of the space-time continuum are slipping—right under your three-dimensional feet! Are you feeling this? The fourth dimension does not adhere to the confines of the space-time continuum, and therefore the appearance of time, as you understand it, simply does not exist there. You can imagine how this complicates your perception of these states of being, and how you cannot measure them, nor relegate them to any relevant framework.

And yet, you do journey the no-time, in states of sleep and astral travel. The difference, perhaps, is that this is occurring now to the entire planet, across the entire solar system, and you are only one of the immeasurable quantum of individuals attempting to understand how possibly ascension can be happening at such a galactic level.

Imagine yourself standing at the shore of the ocean—one foot on the sand, one in the water. You are gazing upon the water's surface, as it appears to you from that vantage point. Let the sand represent the third dimension; let the water represent the fourth.

As you venture out into the water, you cannot help but notice that there is another world entirely, one you barely know, if at all, within the sea. You cannot really see it, and you cannot really interact with it, until you step off the sand and allow the water to engulf you. Immersed, you experience this seemingly familiar environment, this density, so much more differently than as it appeared to you when you were simply looking upon it . . . or splashing around in your comfort zone, but never venturing into the deep of it: never feeling, tasting, seeing it clearly.

There is a completely alien world there, one that you may fleetingly experience more wholly if you dive into its depths, but yet that is not the same as if you could actually breathe there. So you touch upon it, still constrained by your physical limitations and capabilities, yet you remain utterly amazed that this world co-exists on your very own planet. It is a world that precedes the solid earth itself—the great ocean of Gaia, and yet, you barely know it. And, what's more, you can only catch glimpses of it, of all its life and interactive dynamics, because of your physical boundaries as earth-walking, electromagnetic, biological beings.

You cannot help but realize, in such a moment, that, in your perception of your own life and your understanding of the world, you have been missing out on at least seventy percent of a potential field of experience.

Welcome to the fourth dimension!

You, conscious beings of Gaia ascending, are currently residing at the outer "edges" of the fourth dimension, which we remind you is not a place, nor a definable 3D construct, but rather—in terms that most make sense to you, and risking repetition for the sake of emphasis—it is a density. The asphalt jungle that got you there lies far behind you, baking in the sun, cracking from the weight of human constructs.

You have one metaphorical foot on wet sand, the other in water.

From this stance, you are breaching into a field of subtler vibrations, on a spectrum whose expanse is still imperceptible to most human beings . . . but not all. More of you are attuning to fields of frequencies that have heretofore eluded you, and that, we wish to emphasize, is not necessarily climbing "higher," as you understand it—but rather, it is reaching "further." More precisely, we would say that it is about probing more deeply into the nature of existence, breaking through the barriers, refining your experience.

Expanding your capabilities of perception and acclimatizing to frequencies that have always co-existed with your 3D realm (but that have been imperceptible to you) have everything to do with your preparation for ascension into the "higher" realms of refined, subtle energy and harmonious existence—which we intend as the fifth dimension and beyond.

You want the world to change immediately. You want to see, as you have never seen before, and to experience everything from an absolutely conscious viewpoint where there is no longer doubt as to what is unfolding.

Yet, you do surely understand that these gradual shifts are subtle—we have described them to you as so—and that each stage of your progression, through the fourth dimension, will bring new challenges, awakenings, and freedom from the paradigms and conditions of the third.

Time, as you understand it, is melting and slipping out from under you. Beings from other universes are fading in and out, like shadows across an old television screen. Good is being made to appear evil; evil appears good. We see that it has so many of you confused, or leaping wildly from theory to theory, searching for the very ground to which to cling.

It was that ground you held when you were so solidly rooted in the third dimension and the veils were tautly bound around the Earth. However oppressive and denying, there was safety in those constraints upon your consciousness and, although you have longed for this, you may not have anticipated just how wildly you would swing, before the stilling of the pendulum.

It was an opacity deliberately manipulated within you, through the stripping of ninety percent of your DNA, from the time of your inception, when you, twelve-stranded light beings, were seeded on a virgin planet— that so-named "Garden of Eden" that is the Earth.

That was a time when you were absolutely aware that you were seeds of other stars, and of planets far more advanced than yours. You were aware that you were beings of immense light, come to build a world of untold beauty—a three-dimensional "heaven," in a sense—where the light of so many realms would flourish, and go on to manifest the perfected crystal of divine love.

Slowly, that light diminished . . . but never has it gone out.

And now, after the domination of countless civilizations, during which humankind has perpetually ceded its power to those self-imposed rulers who gave you the kings, queens, despots, "leaders," and dictators, you rise again. Faced with your own karma—and that of the collective—you are attuning to the fourth dimension, through which all the layers are woven, and from whence you will take your next steps, or giant leaps, determined not only by your karmic debt, but also by the electromagnetic frequencies that emanate from your mind, body, and spirit.

Those who do not understand, and who have yielded to the fear being inculcated in their minds, are crawling through the haze like terrified newborns. On hands and knees, they tremble at the slightest shiver of Gaia's celestial body. They mourn for what is being taken away, unable to see the new that is being birthed alongside them. And they resonate to those lower vibratory signatures, feeding the ghoulish chimeras of their wildest fears and imaginings.

Those, instead, who are well on their way to understanding the greater scheme of things know that something quite exceptional has occurred: something absolutely unprecedented, monumental, and universal. It is your entire solar body that is raising its pitch, before soaring through its own astral cord and through the anything-but-black hole that will propel it to the higher realms. And it is the planetary beings, like Gaia herself—with all the living, the breathing, and the innocents of her Creation—that are in transition.

Now, at the transference point, whereby you pierce the veils that have shielded so many hidden and unknown aspects of infinite reality from your perception, you are breaking through, or perhaps, more aptly stated, they are merging with your evolving understanding of the multidimensional universe. You are at the outer edges of the fourth dimension, and, as we have elucidated for you since our earliest transmissions, it is not all light and celebration.

Of this you are well aware, as you dodge the chaos that surrounds you, doing your best to maintain your personal and communal equilibrium. As you remove the gauze that has shrouded your vision, you are faced with immensely complex mental constructs that boggle the minds of even the most illuminated. In obvious ways, that stretching of your mind, at the intellectual and experiential levels, is infinitely more daunting than the struggle you see unfolding at this moment. Questioning the illusions that have defined human existence through the millennia, the lies and controls that have been placed upon you, is no longer denigrated as "conspiracy theory," nor the idle contemplation of rebellious visionaries.

In this reference of time, as you understand it to be the few years following the 2012 shift, we have peered through the turbulence that has engulfed your planet, seeking the evolving amongst you . . . and we see your light expanding around the globe, and out into your environs of space. As you struggle to discern truth from fiction, and clarity from fantasy, we are filled with compassion.

Bouncing around between doubt and the trust that hope brings, still you rise.

You rise.

Only fear, being driven into human consciousness with the cruelest, most unacceptable form of weaponry—mind control—can deter you now, if you succumb to it. Not to diminish for a moment our abhorrence of all weaponry against the biology of Earth's ecosystems and all existing beings, we wish to remind you that the manipulated altering of the mind equates to interfering with the sovereign soul imprint that defines your DNA—your nature, and your soul essence. Altering the DNA, as is now under way on every level and in all species, is a deliberate deterrent to sovereign soul intent.

At this level of awareness—your emergence from solid ground, into the etheric waters of the fourth density—you are also contending with energies and their manifestations that reside in the lower frequency range: the shadow beings. They are being released and stimulated by forces that are not of the highest intention and, but for the sightings of ghostly apparitions in so-named "haunted spaces," this aspect, for the most part, has remained hidden to human consciousness—or relegated to some ambiguous brew of horror story-telling that never seems to actually reflect reality. But, now that the veils are lifting, more of you perceive entities on other layers and other time lines. Whether you are personally experiencing such presences, or not, they are nonetheless being evoked and imposed upon the collective consciousness by those we have perpetually referred to as the "dark-intended." This, of course, has everything to do with the struggle of darkness and light playing out in your world.

We simply remind you that it is being orchestrated at other levels, of which you are becoming more aware as you wade through this four-dimensional spectrum. At this density, you are faced not only with the karma of your own persona, your soul's progression, but with the karmic imprinting of the entire planet. That is, you are now being faced with the karma of countless millennia of human existence as the dominant species over all others on the Earth—with all the good and all the wrongs that have been committed. Perhaps, understanding the enormity of that concept, you can understand better why you are in such upheaval at this time.

Be comforted in the knowing that, at the opposite side of that pole, you are also experiencing the extraordinary karma of great masters, artists, and intellectuals, wisdom keepers, elders, and spiritual guardians of the Earth, who anchored light there through those same millennia. Which polar opposite one resonates with, as well you know, is determined by his or her intent, as well as it is by the karmic collection of so many lifetimes. It surely makes perfect sense to you that these demonstrations of such forces—light and dark—are in some way very necessary for the resolution of your own individual and global karmic debt.

That is the challenge before you.

Understand it for what it is, rather than fearing the apocalypse, the End of Days . . . your total annihilation. Your path has led you to observe the collective footprint of all the history of the Earth, as we understand it to be the time *Homo sapiens* has walked upon it, and as you and the planet prepare for the imminent ascension of the entire solar system.

The shadow no longer casts familiar distortions on the ground behind you. Rather, it stands, almost unrecognizable, in front of you, directly—like some cosmic gatekeeper—demanding acknowledgment, healing, and resolution.

We understand that this is a huge undertaking, especially considering how much history there is to forgive and release. Many people, entire nations, do not want to forget or heal the past. They are determined to cling to an identity, an idea of glory or victimization, of which they refuse to let go, killing and willingly dying, in order to perpetuate it.

We have returned to remind you that you are up to the challenge, riding the waves of the cosmic seas. You know how to navigate these waters.

You have traversed the stars, after all . . .

Surely, this.

7

Hope, Empowered

Many of you, starseed and sensitives, are feeling that you cannot bear the pressures of your earthly lives and, increasingly, there is much talk of how you long to escape Earth (a world and a time into which you chose to incarnate) and return to distant star worlds—where you believe you have known much more peace and equilibrium, on every level, and where love for all things flourished.

You are blessed to have known that . . . and you will know it again. But, if your soul mission brought you to experience Earth in the twenty-first century, then here is where you are meant to be—and now is the time for the warrior in you to rise and take back the power you have given to wishing yourself away.

Hope, empowered, is your key.

You are called to create inner and outer peace, in your corporeal form, and through your current vehicles of expression, right now—in the midst of angst, and fear, and the mortal doom that is enveloping human consciousness. You only need to remember that everything that appears to be out of your control does not need to be controlled at all. Instead, seek balance, to re-create the peace you so long for, stilling the pendulum of raging emotions. When you can create that for yourself, you can stand in the middle of a battlefield and feel no fear, knowing that you are immortal, and that the outcome of any and all life-threatening scenarios is change . . . not endings.

That does not mean that there is no suffering, for we know that it is rife on your planet, and we have always spoken openly about it—dissecting it, in order to break it down, into manageable pieces. Why some souls live lives of immense suffering, and others not, remains a question that may never be answered—so vast is it in scope. But what we wish to address, here and now, is how you can transmute suffering, lifting off the weights that have pulled you down into your lower emotions, and soar, once again, past the clouds—and across blue skies.

The transmission of this chapter is especially dedicated to all souls in difficulty, that you can feel our compassion, and be inspired from our vision, thoughts, and concerns.

Believing peace to be an impossible dream for your current planet, and that only by escaping your own planet can you reach a higher state of existence, you unwittingly contribute to the disenfranchisement of the Earth, sabotaging your experience. We know, as do you, that that is not your intention—it is anything but that! However, as disharmony reaches a feverish pitch all around you, you may feel that you are drowning in the collective despair, and so, it is understandable that feelings of hopelessness and alienation seep in, taking over your peace of mind. These negative emotions, in turn, are reabsorbed into the collective consciousness. You have thoughts of quitting the Earth—we hear them, wafting through the ethers. You believe you are ready to leave, by any means: ascension, exoplanetary migration, alien ships . . . even suicidal thoughts linger in the minds of those who are finding it most difficult to cope.

We wish to examine the cause and effect of any mindset that would have you giving up on the Earth, longing to escape it. Let us do that here, boldly and without reservation, so that we can help you remember, when your uncomfortable presence on Earth becomes so clouded in your mind that you simply cannot fathom why you are there at all.

Let us remind you, if you have lost touch with your soul purpose, of who you are, and what you have come to do, on your planet of choice.

No starseed ever accidentally migrates to another planetary environment. It is always a clear and very deliberate choice, and a most courageous one at that, particularly when you have come to assist in some way: as a Bodhisattva, or warrior, or light bearer, shining through the dark alleys and caves of ignorance and fear.

You came with a purpose, determined to contribute to Gaia's process, and to anchor light where light was slowly dimming.

You came to share your vision, your wisdom, and your love.

Let it be that hope, and your soul purpose—clear and resolute— through which you are capable of transforming any acquired doubt, or fatigue. You have only to remember the intent behind your decision to incarnate upon the Earth . . . one precious blue-green planet, struggling to shed its weathered skin, and to be born anew.

The slippery slope that can send you tumbling, from feelings of futility and impotence about your life, to even deeper ones of absolute hopelessness, hurls those emotional triggers into the cellular memory of your experience, planting belief systems that take root quickly and are difficult to release. Thereafter, every cell in your body, vibrating to those frequencies, stores (in some aspect or quantum) a negative mindset: that evil wins over goodness, that hatred is more powerful than love . . . or that darkness obliterates the light. Unless you release the accumulated energies of those emotion-backed beliefs, they perpetually reflect back to your conscious mind, through everything you do, think, and feel—gaining momentum, until, one day, you finally find the way to resolve them, and move forward.

Subject to the illusory construct of space-time, the evolution of those convictions may not be immediately recognizable to you, for there is this aspect to your perception—time—and all things in the physical universe have their own rhythm and pace. It may take time for you to realize those mental constructs: how they are becoming engrained within your mind, and how their degenerative impact can progress—without your realizing it.

However, in the no-time of the fourth density, manifestation is immediate. It will stare you so boldly in the face that you cannot help but recognize your own creations, and deal with them, on the spot. Fear, in any form, will step directly in front of you in the fourth, where it will appear to be far more monstrous than it is in your current framework, cloaked in shadow and nuance, and hidden behind a 3D pillar in your partitioned mind.

What will you carry with you, in your karmic sack? And what can you let go of, here and now?

You do know how your mind can be imprinted, and how easily these images and constructs can be imposed upon the still waters of your subconscious. But, allow us license to reinforce how this mechanism works, and how you can avoid or release it, for your highest good. At this pivotal moment, you are going to be most effective for yourselves, and for the planet, if you are in touch with your emotional body, which is unquestionably assailed by persistent negative imprinting, coming at you from a world in turmoil, and exacerbated through the network. Perhaps we are overemphasizing the obvious; however, we cannot impress upon you enough how important it is to your passage that you be as free as possible from a communication delivery system designed to keep you distracted and anchored to the lower frequencies.

You want to be your most effective now, freed of fear and despair. To be the lightworker you came to be, throughout the earth changes that will culminate in your leap into the next density, you are going to need to take back full possession of your thoughts, in a very determined way. It will mean setting your clear and determined intention to liberate yourself emotionally from everything that upsets your equilibrium—all programs, dogmatic belief systems, and convictions—while still being willing to examine it all, with objectivity.

To be effective, you are called to understand the dark forces, penetrate them with your light, and be fearless before them. The way back from powerlessness and despair is within you. It is not the outside world that is the problem—it is how you experience it, and what you allow to affect you. Step back from the dramas of the social structure—the people, events, and calamities—and recognize that, if you allow anything to overwhelm you to such an extent that it torments you, then you alone have made it your drama, by believing it is a possible reality. And, by making it yours, adding fuel to it, you are feeding its amplified vibration back into the collective.

Negativity, in all its insidious and blatant forms, feeds on lower vibrations and multiplies as rapidly as bacteria—which, as you know, can destroy a healthy host . . . left unchecked and unresolved. You cannot help but notice how negative thoughts, and the raging emotions they incite, cause suffering at the individual and collective levels of your lives. They manifest quickly, infecting individuals susceptible to their force, attacking the lower chakras.

Turned inwards, negativity eventually manifests as physical illness, emotional turmoil, and dependent upon its intensity and duration, it can lead to insanity. When you allow it to rule over your life, exacerbated through your own runaway emotions (particularly your survival fears), you manifest reality that is usually not in your best interest, nor that of the individual subject of your thoughts, your emotions, and your intention.

Turned against others, it can cause incredible pain and suffering to any individual (particularly one who resonates with those lower frequencies) who happens to find her/himself in the firing line. And, as a matter of course, it contributes to the greater dysfunctional society.

Conversely, positivity, borne by the higher vibrations of love and compassion for all things, and for the self, can be more challenging to bring to manifestation, in your current three-dimensional planetary environment—a world in significant turmoil.

You must wonder why we would make such a declaration.

Follow our thoughts.

When you are "hoping," rather than creating positive change for you, for your loved ones, and for all of society—the Earth itself—your focus is still relatively unclear and ambiguous, for the nature of "hoping for change" means that you are still overwhelmed by what is unchanged. You are wishing for it, but not seeing it clearly. You long for change, you dream of a utopic environment, in which to live peacefully, and to raise healthy, happy children, but you are not operating from an empowered state of creation: one of doing . . . and of being.

Unlike the fiery nature of rage, and the magnetism of fear, hope is like still water, deep—but inert. For a body of still water to flow, there must be a powerful energy that activates it—some force that triggers it to ripple, then to surge.

The tiniest pebble, cast into a pond, will cause a quantum of water to ripple outward.

We are simply emphasizing what you already know: that hope, empowered with vision and determination, brings positivity to manifestation. And yet, the dynamic interplay of those essential elements still seems to elude you.

Some fear that acknowledging the existence of negative forces, and of their manifest darkness, dilutes the positive outcome of any intention. We do not see it that way. Before it can be resolved, fear must be acknowledged. You look it straight in the eye, facing it . . . and then, realizing that the monstrous cloud that hangs over you is only a projection of that fear, it dissipates, yielding to the greater emotion of love, which you know you feel inside you.

We are calling you to that power.

Own the power that makes hope manifest, rather than remote and dream-like, and just beyond your reach: unattainable.

That is a tall order; we do understand it. But it is your calling.

It is the way of the New Aquarian.

In contrast to certain disinformation permeating your spiritual communities, constricting you from considering anything but passive contemplation of peace, love, and light, our intention is, and has always been, to help you know truth, within you. It has always been about helping you to pull back the curtain, and to examine the underpinnings of trickery and deceit—so that you understand and disarm them—and be empowered by that knowledge. Any religion, dogma, or teaching that would deny you that wide open field of contemplation is not intent upon your freedom and sovereignty, and we invite you to walk away from it.

We do not subscribe to the blocking of energy in any circumstance, or the building of boundaries, within which consciousness is bound, like a ball and chain, to a predetermined idea. It is our experience, and observation, that such constrictions will always metastasize into an unhealthy and deleterious form of obedience.

Then, too, there is the karmic responsibility that must be acknowledged. The accomplished spiritualist knows that any and all undesirable intent or energy will manifest until it is resolved. Whether underground, dark and murky, or whether it stands boldly before you—it is a force to contend with. The choice not to assist in shedding light upon it, and raising it to a higher vibration, is yours to make. However, we assure you that, by avoiding it, you are actually allowing the undesired outcome to persist, to grow, and to envelop far greater swaths of human consciousness in its wake.

Bring it into the light, where you are free to examine everything that passes over your mind screen, and where you are free to recognize that this monster you are creating there is only a mirage, bubbling up from your subconscious pool, awaiting resolution.

Understanding darkness does not draw you to it—only fear, or one's own attraction to the shadow world, does that. It does not entrain you to those energies, nor to the intention of their source; it merely allows you a broader scope from which to observe the outer world, so that you can examine, objectively and without suffering, its effect upon your inner world. When you recognize how such forces work in opposition to your desired outcome, you will be shown how to dilute the force of their power: to heal them and even to forgive them, which is the ultimate reflection of spirit, made manifest.

Then, and only then, can you step back, reclaiming your sovereignty, and take action that will effect positive change.

Let us arrive at the core issue here, which reflects how you utilize your intellect, your intuition, and the vision of what you want to create now, as you slip in and out of the fourth density, a field within which you will be seeing your intentions become almost instantly manifest, before your eyes.

Instant karmic return is one very significant and recognizable element of the four-dimensional field. You best know how to use your mind to rein in your emotions, so that what you create is what you understand to be in the best interest of all concerned: yourself, your loved ones, and the greater society.

As we have just stated, you will not need to reincarnate to heal karma, because you are going to be facing it, head on, in the fourth density. You will not require many lifetimes of suffering and pain to erase the pain and suffering you inflicted somewhere else . . . some other framework that you identify as a "past life." Similarly, just as that unresolved or disharmonious energy will manifest before you, so will all the good that you have done, and that you continue to create around and within you. That love and compassion will shine before you, illuminating your way, radiating love, and the grace of your compassionate humanity.

This karmic loop is unavoidable; it is simply the way that intent, and the resulting energy that drives it, work. You set an intention, send it out into the ethers, and it comes right back into your personal field of experience. If that intent, thought, or desire is inflated by the communal fear and rage of any others with whom your negative process has interacted, it will only come back to you as a monstrous distortion of that original emotion—that seed. If, instead, your intention is for the good of all, it comes back to you—tenfold.

If you understand karma, you know this to be the result of "cause and effect." That is, you cause something to occur—something that can be as innocuous as a thought that you do not actually act out. At that density, it seeps out into the universal field, and you, and the intended target of that thought or intention, will instantly experience its effect. It will not take lifetimes to learn the karmic lessons from such experience, for there will be no experience of time through which you would need to evolve in order to heal your own deeds and expression. Whatever you create remains in your electromagnetic field, reflecting right back at you, to be integrated into your vibratory signature and emotional experience, which, in so many ways, can be witnessed as your very own angels . . . and demons.

We are saying that you have the opportunity to step off the wheel of reincarnation, and move up the spiral.

There are those of you who, upon reading these words, know and understand that of which we speak. You are the conscious souls who are so aware that you are already experiencing how you are intermittently slipping into the fourth dimension, and then bringing back to the third the experience of instant karmic retribution. It can be sobering, or filled with elation, determined by what you put into the field, and what reflects back to you.

Where do you find the strength and the nourishment to extract yourselves from unwanted emotions? Nature. The perpetual, breathtaking procession of nature, the heart of your planetary deity, is truly the only absolute upon which you can base your perception of reality, for it is the undeniable reflection of Creation, unfolding. Nature is poetry in motion. It is the exquisite—the perfected harmonics of life, revealing mystery upon mystery, in such extraordinary beauty that its mere observation alters the brain waves, imprinting the sacred within the mind, enriching the soul.

It plays the music, colors the tapestry, heals, exalts, and inspires all living beings.

Now that poisons and genetic tampering are mutating the essence of nature on Earth, you are finding it more difficult to experience its pure states—we do understand that. Your urban lives barely glimpse it anymore, so encased are they in steel, cement, and plastic, and all the unnecessary permeations of extreme electromagnetic pollution. But never underestimate Gaia's immense ability to heal and to re-create herself.

Perhaps adaptation and mutations will form, as Gaia finds the way to reestablish balance. There will be armies of bacteria to consume radioactive waste, and others to break down plastic and transmute it—that is simply the way of life. Change is unquestionably upon you, just as it is with nature. You will be wise to escape urban centers, forever, if possible, or for brief encounters, if not—take yourselves, whenever you can, to the deep forest, a meadow, or mountain stream.

Lie in a bed of leaves. Smell the scent of bloom. Feel the wind rustling the boughs of trees. Watch the waves come in and out, crashing on the rocks. There is infinite beauty—and always will be—in Earth's gardens. And that, beloved seekers, is the perpetual expression of hope, empowered through your appreciation of divine artistry, and the observation of its infinite power to re-create itself, in light and beauty.

Gaia, your celestial deity, is pure of intent. No matter how destructive the human drama or alien power games play out, in her fields of being, she will never be destroyed. Do not grieve for her, for she is the master of her immortality. No amount of negativity or abuse can ever subvert her progression—her rightful place in the ascension process—following your sun from its current position (between the third and fourth dimensions) on its way to higher ground.

No matter where you have built your nest in the world, your task, inevitably, is to create beauty, and to choose love over hate, compassion over violence, and the community good over individual desire. And if you believe you are a light warrior, then you know that it means reaching down into the trenches, and pulling the lost and despairing up with you—for they have long forgotten the wisdom of a forest, much less the majesty of a tree.

Knowing truth, in those moments when you truly explore the beauty that surrounds and lies within you, everything else—including the messages you read here—is merely a possible reality. We speak of you, the awakening, when we state that your mind and intellect are constantly weighing a barrage of input, seeking knowledge . . . longing to know what lies ahead. Moreover, we believe you are questioning your mortal existence, the sense of it, and aching to believe, if you still do not, that the soul is immortal.

No matter how things unfold in your world—the good and the bad— you are temporary observers of one level of reality, on your way to another. That is to say, in Sirian terminology, that you are currently resonating to this density and frequency, although you also hold resonance with parallel worlds—even universes of similar yet diverse vibrational essence.

Always remember that this, the reality in which you are able to read these words, is your primary focus for now, but it is not the only one. Far from it.

As always, we invite you to run ideologies, theories, and beliefs, including ours, through your heart, and discard whatever does not ring as truth for you.

You must be exceptionally discerning now, more than you have ever been in the past, if you are to find your way through the marshes of dogma, fantasy, and lies to where you can swim, without fear or judgment, in the clear seas of higher wisdom and unfailing light.

Nature, our understanding of the exquisite, ongoing expression of biology and energy, unfolding everywhere in the multiverse, holds no secrets. Nature leaves no question in the mind of the seeker . . . no doubt, no untold story. You merely have to take time to explore the essence of it, in all its manifestations—from a single cell under a microscopic lens, to the entire oceanic body that covers most of your world—to know that within all the design of Creation is woven infinite intelligence, beauty, and higher consciousness. Nature reminds you that goodness and beauty will always prevail, no matter how great the assault against her, and that life will always seek to regenerate and renew itself.

It is this way upon the Earth, as it is on countless worlds across the heavens.

The forces intent upon impeding Earth can temporarily alter the course of conscious beings—that is certain. You surely see this around you; the mania that is being driven to such frenzy, in the mass mind of your species, is exactly that: driven. Separation is the key to your demise—it always has been. You are being separated and alienated from the music of the Earth, from the animal kingdoms, and from each other—systemically, deliberately, and mechanically—in so many ways.

Fortunately, in the fields of duality, such as those that you are experiencing, there is the other side of darkness: the vision, the awakening . . . the light.

Some choose to bow down to the darkest powers, obeying . . . following . . . subjugating themselves. Paradoxically, others glean greater strength from it, more commitment and determination to heal it. Whatever is happening at the poles of human emotion, remember one essential, indisputable fact: there is no force capable of harnessing Gaia—the Great Equalizer.

Granted, Gaia, the cosmic ship upon which you currently traverse the heavens, is not well, but she always heals. In her current state of dis-ease, she is struggling with several invasive factors that are attacking her immune systems, her regenerative capabilities, and her harmonic resonance, and she is rebelling with every ounce of strength she possesses. You are witness to her raging storms, decaying outer crust, and all manner of violent weather patterns. Some of these are the explosive energies of her rebellion against those injustices being perpetrated against her; others are deliberate manipulations of the secret government, which insists on destroying the spirit of your planet. They are still attempting to lock in a very low frequency for three-dimensional Earth, and, essentially, turning it into a mined fueling station for extraterrestrial merchants of future star wars now being instigated in your sector of the galaxy.

Just remember: nothing will prevent Earth from achieving ascension, for that is your celestial deity's spiritual destiny, one of the many held in the gravitational force of your sun, rising. We ask you always to bear that in mind when you grieve for the Earth and fear your extinction.

Love the Earth. Remember that you were not banished to a prison. You chose to come to a magnificent garden of unfolding experience, knowing that a flower always will bloom there—and you came to plant new seeds. You determine how you will respond to all aspects of your existence—and you determine your vibratory resonance field.

Contemplate your brilliant star, wherever it may be; delight in the wonder of its light, whether it can be seen from this vantage point or not—but honor Earth first. Let there be unconditional love from your heart to hers.

You may have traveled so far to get where you are—isn't that a celebration, of itself? Know that you may very well return, if that is a destiny you wish to create, but for now, Children of the Gaian heart, be the hope and the vision of Earth's evolution.

Stand for hope, empowered.

8

Who Shall Inherit the Earth?

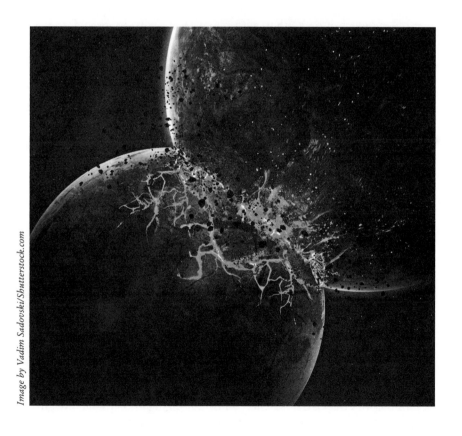

Image by Vadim Sadovski/Shutterstock.com

To elaborate further the imminent process of solar ascension, it is essential that we first dispel an erroneous concept, now circulating via alternative information networks and amongst metaphysical communities . . . and very possibly lingering in your own mind, which we do humbly address here, with due respect and consideration of your free will.

It revolves around the somewhat popular misunderstanding that Earth alone is ascending, and only a part of it, at that. It is a rather curious idea—but then, there are still those who perceive Earth as the center of the universe!

This theory sees your sphere splitting into two separate worlds, forever independent of each other, with two diametrically opposed destinies. In this modern-day rendition of your ancient judgment books, and the values they imposed, the "good" Earth, whereby select souls have made some sort of "grade," and moved up, would be ascending to the fifth or higher dimensions (bypassing the fourth altogether). The other, bound to the darkness of evil beings and unruly hoards of the unenlightened, would be irreparably destroyed, and die a lingering death, deemed its due punishment for all the wrongs that its inhabitants perpetrated in response to their fear, indifference, and violence . . . and taking all those souls deemed "unworthy" down along with it.

After so many millennia, this rhetoric, no matter how it has been redressed, should sound familiar to you. Although the terminology has changed, it is the replay of an established paradigm: heaven versus hell, good against evil, and reward over punishment. The parameters of the judgment system, whereby a force outside of you deems you worthy or not, have been rewritten into a new script, but it is the same ancient story, a tried and tested tale of religious fervor, which, to this day, is intent upon controlling entire societies into determined behaviors. It imposes guilt and chastisement through systematic rules over moral conduct, and the salvation of the soul through obedience, while impinging upon the sovereignty of one and all beings. It allows no tolerance for any other belief system but its own, and incites human spirit to destroy, torture, and kill, in the name of its self-serving, righteous principles, and the established godhead of choice.

As an aside, and digressing, for a moment, from the discussion of the split-Earth theory, we remind you that it is religion that is being used to stir irrational behaviors and hatred between you. An unholy war is in place, deliberately and methodically imposed upon you, in order to render you subservient, and accepting of punishment imposed by its self-appointed minions.

It is a branch of the secret government.

Fanatic religion has always been and always will be the most powerful behavior modification tool of the authority, for it churns at your very sense of existence, and pretends to know all answers to the questions of what is happening inside you, and what events are outside of your control. It tells you that it alone knows God, and that its narrative is the only true story of Creation. Everything outside the confines of its dogma is a lie, and all who do not bow down to its command are infidels, and hence enemies, by default.

The judgment system inherent in almost all religion has carried over into variations on earlier themes, through creative interpretations from your metaphilosophers who attest to the existence of two primary parallel time lines: one positive, where Earth flourishes—the other negative, where darkness accelerates out of control, taking everything with it, through endless suffering, on the way to a violent, scorching death.

With what you know of energy, resonance, and the oneness of all things, won't you agree that the idea of Gaia, the nonjudgmental, quintessential mother, behaving in such a way as to determine which human beings are worthy, and which are not, is at the very least questionable? You surely cannot believe that the exquisite and bountiful soul of your planet is capable of such judgmental parenting, serving up punishment and condemnation for the unworthy souls that have not attuned to a high enough frequency to take part in their home planet's evolution.

Ask yourself this: would any celestial being, as beautiful as Gaia, one that exhibits such an incredible spectrum of light and vital life force, condemn any part or reflection of herself to perennial darkness, or destruction, and finally—to her own demise? In other words, are you to believe that there can never be healing of darkness, and resolution of polarity?

What of the children? Would they be judged for their potential evil intentions, or inappropriate behaviors? And of other life forms on the planet—what of them? Which ill-fated animals would be thrown to the wolves? Which would be free to roam the new, unblemished Earth: the return of the Garden of Eden? Which birds, what flowers and trees would be scorched in the evil fires of hell, and what others would be graced with a heavenly world, where good reigns, unblemished and shining, like a sculpted diamond in the heavens?

Noah's twenty-first-century Ark has already left for Mars, carrying the DNA of every species of flora and fauna, so perhaps that is not a consideration for the dichotomy of the two-Earth hypothesis.

This theory of Earth, divided, does not represent the multidimensional universe, as it would have you believe. No doubt there exists a parallel Earth, whose outcome is reflective of the synthesis of "evil," for there is always a great spectrum of energies on the material plane, but we do not see Earth twinning into two polar aspects of itself, whereby all humans have earned either their reward or their punishment.

This just does not fit the design of cosmic progression.

There is not now, and never will there be, an evil Earth that has separated from a strictly good, purely loving Earth, in polar opposition. This concept reflects convictions, still carved into certain individuals' consciousness, that people are basically good or evil. That is such a very limited way of looking at the world, for there is a constant rebalancing of vibrations in your lives, weighing the values of your own morality against those that are imposed upon you. Inevitably, there are light and dark reflections perpetually seeking resolution in your soul, just as they are in the souls of others.

Gaia, the celestial deity and spirit essence of Earth, is integral. Through so many billions of years of her own physical presence in the material universe, she has nurtured life, and exalted its magical imprint upon her own body. She does not fear the shadow; she heals it. You will never see an evil blade of grass. There is only growth, in its cyclical experience, birthing, blooming, waning, and passing—burying its seed, for the season that follows.

And then, the cycle repeats . . . and then again . . . and again . . . and again.

Nothing short of a thermonuclear holocaust—an all-out, final war that is so ferocious it literally blows the planet apart—can possibly destroy the Earth. Were such a scenario to occur, in a solar system that was not ascending, those hypothetical bits and pieces would be ejected out into space, and would slowly, over time, mutate, evolve, and rebirth the seed of life, and the spirit carried through it. Were it to occur in the near future, before you ascend, these same parcels of Earth would simply experience themselves in another form or design, where they would face the karma of what caused them to separate, and they would heal, much more rapidly, once that karmic responsibility had been resolved.

Children of Gaia, if you still have not had your fill of heaven and hell scenarios, and if you are looking to re-create them in a future context—for yourselves, or for humanity at large—search no further than your own experience: your memories, the emotions with which you carry them forward, and your relationship to Earth itself.

If you dream of a heavenly utopia, create it now—observe it, memorize it, and live it, with your heart wide open. It is woven into the tapestry of nature, if only you will stop to listen to the sounds of birdsong, and to smell the flowers. Spend more time in the woodland, or walking along the shore, far from the urban jungle, and away from programs that push you into fear and hopelessness.

If, instead, you are determined to follow fear, and to fear hell, well . . . we shall not invite you to create that! Just remember that you create your own reality, and you carry it with you, entrained to its vibration. What happens then, to each of you, is determined by your own vibratory attunement and determination.

We understand and perceive that there are several Earths, existing simultaneously, similar to each other to such a point that they can be indistinguishable, one from the other. You exist in all of them, in parallel lives, experimenting with different choices and their outcomes, similar to those that challenge you in this, your perceived "primary" reality. There is no distinctly negative or absolutely positive time line for Earth, or for any other planet, even for any universe—and hence, knowing what we have discussed of macro- and microcosms, how could there be for any one of you?

Projecting three-dimensional polarity, in all its extremes, into a new landscape—a planet physically divided into two separate worlds—does not represent the nature of reality as we understand it, and, therefore, we do not endorse this theory.

What we do see ahead of you, similar to the two (or more) "time line" theories, honors the sovereign soul purpose of every living being to progress to higher states of consciousness, as a reflection of the choices it has made on the way. Some prefer to cling, obstinately, to the lure of the shadow lands; others cannot wait to leap ahead, knowing that the light gets brighter at the top of the stairs.

Karmic restitution is yours to make. Do not allow it to be imposed upon you by a judgment committee, or lesser gods. Some will pause to reflect upon what a soul brings to the lifetime, and the life place, and what it takes with it when it passes from form. Others will not understand, clutching hard and fast to their demons.

No matter where your focus lies, you will always carry Earth with you.

The beauty, the ugliness . . . the wisdom of some, the ignorance of others, the suffering—all of this is who you are, as children of the Earth, and all of it is a reflection of your process.

Nothing gets left behind.

How it is dealt with, in the karma windows of the fourth dimension, is something each individual will be faced with, just as you, as a civilization, are already confronting now—in the flutter and on the wings of your merging realities.

9

Parallel Universes

A Cosmic Hall of Mirrors

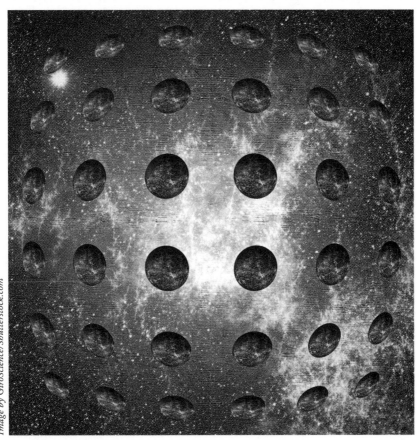

We reiterate that there exist several Earths, occurring simultaneously, across the universe of matter. They exhibit several degrees of diversity, in an expanse of many parallels that exist as three-dimensional, planetary stations there. And they co-exist, simultaneously, as various frameworks, in different degrees of reality. These worlds are just as physical as yours; they are almost twins to yours—where diverse cause and effect scenarios play out alternative responses to stimuli, on every level. Each has a different evolutionary pace, but relative to the one you most likely perceive as the only one, and each offers different outcomes to your personal and social issues.

You believe your primary existence is the one that has you reading this information—right now: Planet Earth, calendar time 2017. Yet, is it not possible that what you are experiencing now is a reflection of another reality, in which all is more harmonious, and living peace? On the other hand, can it be that there exists a simultaneous Earth where there has been a devolution of society, and all is declining far more rapidly than it appears to be on Earth Station Central?

As you become increasingly aware of the multiverse of co-existing realities, in simultaneous time, you are free to contemplate countless scenarios where you exist in different forms, in different environments, and with options that span an infinity of possibilities.

We are stating that you, a multidimensional being, co-exist in parallel worlds, simultaneously. You do live parallel lives, experimenting with different challenges, opportunities, and choices that you respond to, or create, in this, your perceived "primary" reality. So do your loved ones, including the animals you protect and nurture, exist in and respond to an infinite array of similar situations and environments that co-exist in those same simultaneous worlds to yours.

Contrary to several hypothetical interpretations of time and the space-time continuum, there is no predetermined negative, or absolutely positive, time line for Earth or any other planet . . . or star . . . or galaxy! However, there are degrees, fields of opportunity, in which possible realities play out, on what you may understand to be different "time lines," running along the galactic conveyor belts that define the space-time continuum. These are laced throughout the physical universe, propelling everything in a sort of cohesive futuristic or past construct, which is more accurately described as a "forward and backward" perspective . . . but that is still far from accurate. To describe the indescribable, we hope to bend those linear terms with which you are familiar, in order to illuminate and speak in terms that are relative to, but not limited to, your experience.

When you are still rooted in the third dimension, it is nearly impossible to perceive that there exist no future and no past—that there is only concurrent, simultaneous experience. We do understand that, and we grapple with how to catapult you past it, at least for the sake of this discourse, pushing your perception off the conveyor belts of space-time.

Mental institutions are filled with individuals diagnosed as psychotic, described as being afflicted with "multiple personality disorders," or schizophrenia. Consider that while, of course, some of these individuals are ill, and delusional, others are not actually mentally ill at all—at least not in the classic sense of what mental illness means to that field of "medicine."

Rather, some individuals, for whatever reason, have an open door in their minds where they perceive themselves, concurrently, in these parallel worlds, and it is so overwhelming that, understandably, they cannot hold focus in any given reality. Therefore, they experience themselves, simultaneously, as different aspects, or personalities, of their core essence.

We are declaring that not all those condemned as medically or psychologically insane are ill in such terms, and that, rather, they are capable of jumping from one parallel life to another, but are unable to anchor themselves enough, in any one of these, to be able to cope with the pressures of social responsibility, and their own conscious awareness.

Image by Mayer George/Shutterstock.com

Further, we wish to suggest that you, too, leap from one parallel life to the other, but that you most often manage this in the dream state, so that it does not disrupt your conscious perception in the alpha and beta states of awareness, and so that you can carry on your relationship to your environment, without being completely disoriented—lost between worlds.

This basic precept defies everything you believe about your daily life, with all its time references: natural or cyclical ones, such as the seasons, and man-made attempts to define every minute, through clocks and calendars, throughout history.

Terms such as "parallel lives" and the "no-time," and other references to conscious states beyond the 3D reference zone, erase your sense of history. They bring into question the past-life/reincarnation tenet as well, and that is truly challenging, for even the most expansive minds.

Is your perception of a past life an expression of time, or is it that you still exist, in a framework that appears to be historical in nature, in a parallel world . . . where that situational environment is still in play? Is reincarnation actually the soul's progression to a new experience, or is it the mere transference of a predominant, conscious focus to a simultaneous one?

These existential questions are mind-boggling to the philosopher, and, no doubt, you, too, struggle with them. We, ourselves, refer to peaks and valleys in your "history," and hence, it appears we contradict ourselves when we tell you that past and present—linear time—are illusions, and that what you perceive, as either, exists, somewhere, in the framework of simultaneous realities and parallel worlds.

Throughout the expanse of human existence, there have been skilled time travelers who have managed to manipulate the space-time continuum, jumping from one simultaneous reality to another—and returning with all manner of experience and information.

Some go insane.

Others, military technicians, have been trained to step into the "future," and return with technologies and insights that have catapulted society forward, and sometimes backward—from moral and ethical points of view. Engineering does exist that facilitates that process, and you will be witness to it, in the very near future. There do exist "time machines" that are actually capable of altering the space-time continuum, and we leave it to your imagination to postulate what that would mean to the curious time traveler. They have to do with the reorganization of the subatomic substance of space, which is not unlike what occurs in the microwave oven. When you change the subatomic organization of space, you create a temporary warp in the continuum, altering time, which facilitates how you breach to other worlds.

Sometimes it is the case that designated time travelers step to the ultimate brink of what you would call your civilization's "past" (but which obviously still exists if they are capable of walking there), when societies, such as that of dark Atlantis, had mastered the unimaginable. This was particularly exalted in their development of mind-control technologies, which have been delivered into the present, and which are being utilized against all peoples, in varying degrees, everywhere around your world. Those towers that have gained dominance over the terrains of your populated regions utilize microwave frequencies that pass through you, effectively overstimulating your molecular structure, altering your body and mind, and damaging your DNA. This is just one of the technologies that has come through the time machines of such travelers.

There is a reason why highly technological moments in your history have been followed by the unbridled destruction of civilizations that used the technological manipulation of time to impact the sovereignty of other nations and societies, and the Earth itself.

You have only to consider the peaks and valleys of human evolution to realize that power swings from dark to light and back again, repeatedly, across the ages, or that technology catapults you forward at times, back to the wastelands of your own destruction at others, and so on and so forth . . . in perpetuity . . . sweeping civilizations. Whether this monumental pendulum is pulled by time (as you understand it), or whether it is set in motion by intervention from more technologically advanced marauders from space, what matters is that you recognize that what you have been led to believe about the past is pretty much the design of those who wish to control you. And from this, you can only deduce that they most likely have similar intentions regarding your perception of the future, and of what you are becoming.

We are not technicians, and we do not interfere with your sovereignty. We have already declared that intention to you, at the onset of this work, and it is a theme that threads through each transmission. Let that be a very clear distinction, for you to hold to the light of the highest truth and to your personal discernment.

From the time of your seeding upon your Earth, we have observed and interacted consciously and energetically with those of you who are attuned to a higher frequency—on different levels—from other dimensions, or more precisely, other densities, interrelated to your present reality. And if we deem it important to help you to understand time travel, or mind travel, such as that which catapults astral explorers through the ethers, it is expressly intent upon opening your own conscious minds to the greatness of the human spirit—rather than harnessing of information that can be brought back to dominate it.

Why this occurs is unanswerable. "How" it does is the question upon which we hope to shed light, and to ease some of the confusion that surrounds it, enough so that you can recognize and distinguish parallel worlds from co-existing dimensional frameworks: the physical universe on the one hand, and the greater, multidimensional universe, through which matter is made manifest, on the other.

Always bearing in mind that you are the microcosmic representation of the macrocosm, remember that whatever exists in the multiverse is within you, within every cell of your being, and that, similarly, everything that exists in your body and your spirit essence is the absolute nature of the Cosmos. This is so difficult for most of you to understand, because you do not relate to the subatomic world—whether you understand it intellectually or not. You do not follow the interaction of protons, electrons, neutrons, and such—they are irrelevant to your day-to-day existence, in the denser realm of your lives. Still today, you do not possess the tools to properly observe the dance of particles and waves, for there is no technology that can see beyond the minute, the infinity that lies outside of it—and of course, there is no way to compartmentalize and dissect the consciousness that causes energy to interact—at any level.

Neither at the other end of the spectrum, beyond the physical universe, with its spinning elements—the macrocosmic dance—does there exist equipment that can measure the consciousness that creates matter: the space between particles, galactic frequencies, waves, gravity. Do you see that, at either extreme, beyond your three-dimensional experience of life, is found the same exact substance—operating in differing proportions—and that you, and your world, are of that identical essence and dynamic energy? A being of biological substance, you are the unfathomable quantum in relationship to a subatomic particle. You are the immensity to the microscopic world; you are the minute to the Cosmos . . . but everything that exists is of the same substance and energy, in varying proportions. Within and beyond the minutiae of the subatomic realm, and the enormity of the multiverse, is found the same field of possibility, conscious potential, and the absolute nature of all Creation, which is simply **to exist.**

While, clearly, the focus of our interface with you is to help you prepare for the shift into other dimensional levels of consciousness, we believe there is much you can glean from understanding parallel physical worlds, and how you actually play a similar role in more than one play. Anything that can help you find your way through the haze of uncertainty, or mere curiosity, we are eager to provide. Contemplation of the fiber of the universe of matter, in any way that takes your mind to thoughts of galactic proportions, will help you take the next leap—to the cosmic measure, if it can be even considered in the same terminology.

Almost two decades ago, through our deliverance of perspectives on simultaneous worlds that resulted in our third book of revelations, we shared with you introductory perspectives on parallel realities. Our transmitter asked that we "step down" the complexity of our information at that time. What we shared then, and what we believe is salient to our further elaboration in this context, is as follows:

> A scent can transport you to a simultaneous reality because within the patterns of consciousness of that smell are vibrational frequencies upon which your minds ride, like surfers on the waves, to that alternative experience instantaneously. A sound wave can similarly strike a resonant chord within your cellular patterning that aligns every cell of your being with the frequencies that occurred in that moment—vibrations that are in tune or resonant with parallel universes in which you do also exist—and so it is that every time you hear that sound it will always transport you to that reality. It serves as the vehicle upon which you are capable of traveling to that experience, and it will be resonant to you forever.

A given lifetime, reflecting back to you all the cosmometric patterns laced through it, is as such resonant with you eternally, which is how you journey back and forth in "time," in space, across the galaxies. Not only do you journey to observe these realities—you do exist within them, and therefore you do utilize those experiences to effect new outcomes continually.

—*No More Secrets, No More Lies: A Handbook to Starseed Awakening,* Book Three of the Sirian Revelations Trilogy (Berkeley, CA: North Atlantic Books, 2008).

What we were intent upon expressing at that time was that, by nature of your co-existence in parallel worlds, you do affect each of them, or shall we say—they affect each other. It is not unlike observing yourself in a hall of mirrors, where your image bounces around in countless reflections—with the exception of one very significant fact. You know that those reflections are dependent upon your standing there, in front of the primary mirror. But what if the reflection in one of those glassy plates actually performed independently? If you were to see a subtle difference in each of those reflections, then you would be witness to a very accurate depiction of your existence, mirrored throughout the physical universe, in parallel worlds.

As you can glean from these pages, filled with complicated theory at times and, hopefully, resonant ideas at others, parallel worlds in physical space are another conceptual conundrum altogether from that of varying densities—the dimensions. Dimensions are not parallel in that way, although they do, of course, reflect aspects of a soul's essence. But, just to differentiate between these two distinct states of being, we can say that you may be a six foot tall human in the third dimension, in one or more parallel worlds, but in the sixth dimension, you would most likely be a ball of light!

As for the world itself—your planet, and your place in it—know that Gaia will remain a part of you throughout eternity, just as you will always be a part of her. You never leave behind an experience of yourself: all that you glean from your environment, and all you give to it. So, be aware of your interface with every aspect of nature, all living beings, and the air you breathe—because you take it with you. All of it is part of you, forever.

Everything imprints your DNA—that architecture of consciousness, manifesting matter, reflecting the soul essence—in all its measure, and that stays engraved on the soul, when spirit lifts out of form. Whether you choose to bring forward the beauty, or whether you choose to carry the baggage of pain and suffering, is a choice only you can make, but do always remember how everything becomes your karmic legacy.

Make life beautiful, loving, and compassionate, and you will bring that to any and all experience; make it dark and filled with fear, and it will haunt you.

Are you a starseed voyager, desperate to return to your home in the stars? Do you really want to remember your current world, your planet of choice for this lifetime, as a place you loathe and wish you never had lived? Believing your star was so much more advanced, will you roam the Cosmos, seeking a better world, only to realize that making a better world was your reason for coming to Earth to begin with? From loathing and resenting your life there, are you prepared to transmute those emotions to carry forward her breathtaking beauty: her fountains, the forest, the eyes of a doe . . . a child's laughter?

What is your vibrational signature? Do you cling to fear and your disillusionment with a life you believe has not fulfilled you? Can you be terrorized into submission, allowing media and programming to destabilize your thoughts, shaking you from your foundation? Or do you choose love? You will find resonance with either emotional pole on your three-dimensional planet, for it offers a broad spectrum of possible realities from which you can decide where you are going to anchor yourself. Understand that your task, from the spiritual perspective, is to raise your vibration, while you are still there—working to heal yourself, and rise to the higher end of the spectrum.

In that hall of mirrors, even the minutest difference in dimension, the texture of the glass, its imperfections, even the variations in light will slightly alter . . . even deform . . . the image represented within it. Moreover, and perhaps most importantly of all, you will notice that as soon as you take your primary focus to another mirror, the one before you distorts, blurs, or somehow warps your experience of your own reflection.

Everything depends upon where you place your focus.

You stand there, observing yourself, primarily, in the mirror directly in front of you, although your peripheral vision allows for glimpses of other sides of you—other perspectives. And all those other reflections—how are they the same, and how are they different?

What do you see?

That energy, your light or darkness, the imprint of a lifetime of joyful anticipation or unfulfilled expectations, refracts through the dimensions, and plays out in worlds you have yet to realize are mirrors of your own.

Surely that gives you pause to reflect upon what a soul brings in to the lifetime and the life place, and what it takes with it, when it moves on.

10

Stargates, Wormholes, and Portals

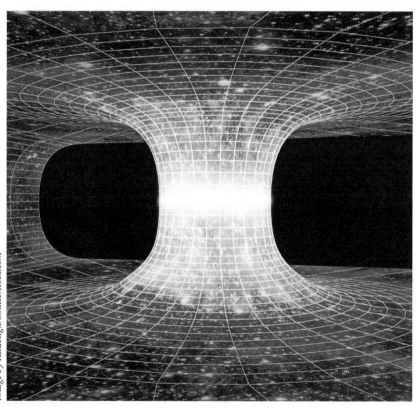

The spirit of your expanding physical universe pushes through its
 vortices,
journeying on astral planes, to experience its higher dimensional
 selves,
as well as the parallel universes
which co-exist as deity bodies of Prime Creator.

— *The Cosmos of Soul: A Wake-Up Call for Humanity*

Now that quantum physicists are beginning to understand the true nature of black holes, and how they lead to other dimensions, we wish to elucidate how immense are the passageways, tunnels, and tubes that traverse the physical universe itself—the space of matter—and how they expand, contract, are birthed, and wither in the face of intelligent design and intent.

We can agree that the form and substance of physical space, the "material" universe, is still so foreign to you. As physical inhabitants of a three-dimensional world, you still regard matter as solid, dense stuff—with borders, finite edges, and individuality. And so, applying that perception to the galactic realms, beyond your planet, or even to the subatomic field, you are understandably struggling with the question of the "in-between"—those enormous distances between planets, star systems, moons, and all other celestial life forms that inhabit your quadrant in space and beyond.

Although they are slowly opening to the possibility of a divine design to the universe, your operatives in all phases of space exploration still have not entirely embraced the fact that space itself is not a void. Rather, it is a wholly conscious, interacting energy field, constantly altered by the intentions, thoughts, and consciousness of every being within it. Space is neither uniform nor stable. All is in a perpetual state of evolution, interaction, and mutation. Every celestial form, every sound each emits, and every thought that rides the waves of the unified field affects the quality, the density, and the formation of space.

We have elucidated how that applies exactly to the subatomic world, the microcosmic representation of the greater universe in which atoms that are just as distant, relatively, from each other, as stars are from other stars, and how they utilize energy to create form—and to alter the space between them.

The material universe is not impenetrable. Planets and stars are not actually divided by insurmountable distances, nor is space the unforgiving environment that it has, for so long, been depicted to be, to interested human audiences. Rather, it is a thriving metropolis of galactic highways, with their entrances, exits, and thoroughfares, and where the laws of earth-based physics barely apply.

It is a field of boundless opportunity, where what appears to be constrained by time and distance can actually cause both to contract, to expand, or to bend, according to intelligent design and conscious intent.

There are multitudinous beings, across the expanse of that space, capable of just that! Some are peaceful and co-creative; others are warring and perpetually destructive. Whatever their focused intention, they are capable of altering space, as a means to traverse it effortlessly, and your own explorers are at the breakthrough point of acquiring that ability. In fact, in the immediate future of your life on Earth, the military-based probing of space will have acquired the capabilities needed to create portals, and to open tunnels and tubes in the physical matrix.

But unless they learn humility, and seek peaceful exchange, what resonant frequencies will they attract at the end of their passageways, and just what will they bring to the other side of the Milky Way?

If you wish to understand how true motion and propulsion manifest in space, through the universal grid, you must first learn to explore your own physical realm, reminded that the greater universe, the macrocosm, is, by nature of all reality, one and the same as the microcosmic representation of all Creation. If you speed up subatomic elements, achieving a frenzy of energetic activity, matter heats up and expands; if you slow it down, the opposite occurs—cooling and constricting.

Master this, and you master travel through space.

You need to know how to alter the subatomic makeup and the behavior of matter—something like microwaving the space in front of your craft, cooling and constricting the space behind. This is how a ship can be made to jettison forward, or backward, at will; it is more about altering space than it is about the craft itself.

Movement, in any direction, can be manipulated by utilizing technology that simply alters the space around a craft. So, when you see an unidentified flying object take a ninety degree turn in the night sky, know that this is the exact method its navigators are utilizing to propel their craft. Since no organization on Earth has yet acquired that capability, you can pretty much consider (for the moment, at least) that ships that are exhibiting such navigational dexterity are of unearthly origins.

By nature of that process, it is clear that the deliberate expansion of space, in a given direction, will create tunnels, or tubes, through which to travel, although it is also the case that tunnels, or valves, in space can exist as a naturally occurring phenomenon of the field.

All biological forms exhibit some form of intake and elimination tubes in their construction. Your own physical being is a continuum of tubes, tunnels, and cords: blood, lymph, food intake and elimination tubes, and neural highways. Energy passes through the tubular constructs of your bodily systems, for the purpose of moving energy, of nourishing every aspect of your being through biological intake, and of releasing all unnecessary waste. This is how your bioelectromagnetic form keeps vital parts of you alive and aware . . . and how it removes parts that have deteriorated or died, needing to be sloughed off, for the well-being and proper maintenance of the overall mechanism.

Your lives are seed of the father, passing sperm through the urethral tube into the vaginal tube, where it is carried to the fallopian tubes of the mother, to fertilize the ovum. From there, the fertilized egg gestates until the hour of birthing, at which time the new life passes back through the birth canal, and is delivered to the outer world.

Contrarily, in death, the spirit leaves the material shell of the body, or cellular form, through the crown, journeying the astral cord through the ethers, and onto its next stage of development, which can be another dimension, another incarnation (though there is usually a time of rest and rejuvenation between lives), or, for some, a place of nebulousness, where the soul is trapped between dimensions, worlds, forms, or lives. This, the grey zone, also exists as a tunnel, from which trapped souls struggle to find the exit portal.

Lava tubes form natural passageways to allow for volcanic flow. Animals burrow tunnel passageways: some, like sea creatures, create them as protective housing, in the deep, hungry sea.

Man has borrowed from nature and learned how to move water, waste, and energy through tubes and pipes that traverse the air, the surface, and the below of your world. Transport systems move people in the underground, from place to place, faster and more efficiently than surface transport. Tubes are riddled through the subsurface, where your military/ corporate/political engineers have carved out tunnels from one coast to another, serving to transport individuals, food supplies, air systems, and— of course—weapons.

Is it any more difficult to visualize, then, a universe that can be traversed through tunnels, tubes, and gateways that are the conscious creation of life itself: of the intelligent design and expressed need of beings who have mastered the nature of multidimensional reality so acutely that they have managed to engineer intergalactic highways—shortcuts through space? Consider how much more efficiently people are transported by subway systems, designed as tubes that cut across the obstructions, clutter, and chaos of surface roadways.

Tubes or tunnels in space are not simply arbitrary energy vortices or portals, although these do naturally exist there. Instead, they serve as constructs carefully designed by intelligent species moving about, planet to planet, star system to star system, with greater speed, ease, and convenience than that which is currently being presented to the human race as "space travel." Some of these are relatively fixed, while others are the temporary passageways of extremely knowledgeable astronauts and space engineers.

If you were a miniature traveler, trying to get from one side to another of a hunk of Swiss cheese, would you choose to painstakingly burrow through the density of the matrix, or would you simply pass through one hole to another, until you reached the exit? If you had to get from one side of the city to another in record time, would you set out in the dense traffic, where you know passage is inhibited by all manner of obstruction, or would you jump onto a subway train and emerge on the other side of your city? We shall say that it is energetically economical to take the shortest path from one point to another; that is the simple, yet often overlooked, paradigm of the construction of such tunnels—in all fields, in all realms, and in all universes.

How your government portrays space travel to your current societies, and how they negate extraterrestrial visitation, is found in their limited understanding of infinite space and dimension, one in which distances between worlds are portrayed as insurmountable or, at least, out of reach for intergalactic contact. You are shown antiquated models of ships requiring monumental thrust to break away from Earth's magnetic force, traversing relatively close distances, and then returning home.

The truth is that your space teams are well beyond such futile exercises. They achieved time travel before your second global war, and with what they have retrieved from "the future," they are propelling human civilization forward technologically, to their desired point of deliverance, whereby they believe they have seen Earth become a robotized, lifeless mining station in space.

It is of the utmost importance that you read this next sentence with absolute attention and the clearest focus. What these military time travelers do not understand is that, actually, they have not traveled to the future, and they are not witness to the future of Earth—as they believe it. Rather, they have traveled to a simultaneous Earth, where such a scenario has already taken hold—and one that is resonant to their belief systems, and programming. Perhaps, if you are willing to stretch your imagination, you will realize that it is their own thirst for that end that has helped create it in the parallel or mirror world to yours.

What we can tell you, with absolute certainty, is that no tubular construct exists, in any state of being—in any dimension—unless it is there to serve the express purpose of functioning as a designated matrix through which energy passes from one space, or specific density, to another.

Answers to the questions of where a wormhole or tunnel in space leads, and what awaits it at the other end, lie in the intent of the explorer, commercial traveler, or invading force.

There is such an infinite possibility of parallel universes and other dimensions. Surely you can imagine the breadth of diversity that exists between them. And if you can imagine your own world and your place in it, reflected in other universes, then you would be on track contemplating how you would appear and function within them. You would note that, in some of these reflections of your conscious existence, there are all manner of possible realities playing out, like some infinite reality show that knows no end of seasons.

The laws of physics, as you know them, may not apply, at least not entirely . . . perhaps not at all. Therefore, the conventional scientists' views of black holes and their impossible, crushing gravitational force are, at the very least, one-sided.

This is quite a conundrum for the scientists who try to define gateways, passageways, and astral cords through space. They may know (or think they know) the forces that operate at their side of a wormhole, but they do not understand where it leads, how it functions, and how it presents at the other end.

Does it lead to a universe where gravity does not exist?

Does it push energy, or matter, such as that of a planetary being, into a new domain where the structure exists in a light body, or less dense version of itself?

Is it just as possible that, like a superhighway, this tube or tunnel splits into one or more secondary tubes, like a cosmic fork in the road, allowing whatever is drawn to move through it with free will choice as to its next density or expression?

We invite you to consider that highways that slice through space and time lead to several diverse experiences of reality. One, perhaps the least difficult for you to perceive and to contemplate, is a realm, let us say a parallel universe, in which the laws of existence are quite similar to yours. Now, take a leap in your imagination to visualize another universe where they are not, where few, if any, of your laws (or at least your interpretation of them) apply—defying space-time, defying gravity, defying your very nature, at the subatomic level.

Finally, and here is our point: imagine multiple universes in which aspects of one are reflected, in varying degrees, as countless other expressions of existence. We speak here of any and all realities that can exist within, between, and beyond others—realities we, too, have yet to discover . . . realities that, perhaps, are not meant to be known to conscious beings, for reasons that could have to do with the mysterious underpinnings of the multiverse.

Of course, we want to know what it all means.

We are very aware that we are most effective when we stretch ourselves beyond limitation, without distorting our wisdom with wild imaginings of the yet unknowable forces, of what we like to call "Creator's Mathematical Hyperverse." This is where anything can exist and can be altered, where anything can be present but not past or future, and where matter and antimatter, dark and light, interplay, creating fields of opportunity for us all to grow. Throughout these levels of possibility, only one truly makes sense universally—and that is that all is conscious, all is eternal, and all is subject to some yet unknown laws of Creation that may never be disclosed to us: no matter how far we climb the spiral, no matter how vast our explorations of space, reality, and dimensions.

As for the multidimensional universe, these are cords of a different matter. The elite and their warriors do know about wormholes to other universes, but they do not understand astral cords and how spirit ascends, for they have lost their spirit on the way to perennial war.

These are not constructs in space—rather, they are a soul's own creation, and only spirit, reaching higher, journeys there. This is the case of your sun.

You, who are drawn to our vibration, know you are connected to higher realms through astral cords that run through your crown, reaching out to the heavens. There are also energy pathways running from your soles, reaching down into the planetary bio-fields—to draw the love of Gaia into your being, and to ground you in Earth's magnetic force and mineral nourishment. They serve to draw universal consciousness into your cells, your subatomic fields, and your mind . . . but also outwards, where you share your illuminated soul with the greater light that is the higher good.

These same cords run through the solar crown and into the higher realms—as do yours. They are not navigational hollows for space travel— they are the vibrational cords through which matter passes to that state of being "less dense," described (in previous passages) as a manifestation of spirit, ascending.

They can lead to far more complicated realities than the one in which you are present, just as they can open into fields of immense light, harmony, and peaceful co-existence. Remember that you take Earth with you.

You, who have blossomed in Gaia's embrace, take your earthly experience, and all the memories, with you.

Whether your journey has been one of struggle, or of peace, the question remains: what will you carry through the astral cord of your sun, to be held up to the light of your next experience?

11

Your Star's Magic, Mutation, and Song

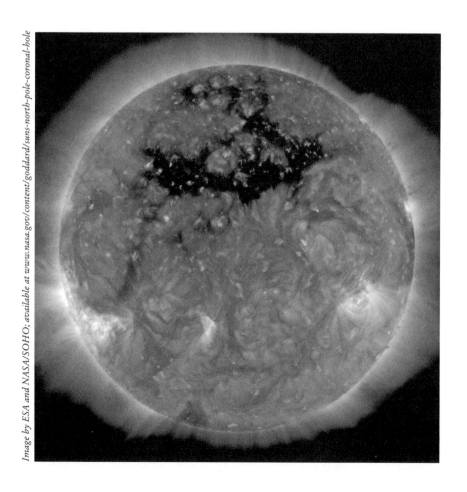

Image by ESA and NASA/SOHO; available at www.nasa.gov/content/goddard/suns-north-pole-coronal-hole

Imagine . . . just as shimmerings of fiery brilliance
exploding out as radiance of your Solar Deity and, slowly cooling,
take form as celestial bodies in your solar system,
so does all consciousness
break from the light, and
in descending into physical reality
take on the "crust" or outer shell of the physical body.

—*The Cosmos of Soul: A Wake-Up Call for Humanity*

It is our purpose, in this missive, to provide a glimpse of your sun's transmutation, from the perspective of our six-dimensional observation stations, beyond the universe of matter. We observe how the flutter of four-dimensional reality appears to brush up against the space-time continuum, slowing you down at one intersection, and speeding you up at another.

We see portions of the sun, slipping into the fourth, and back out again, into its electromagnetic plasma body—and we are not speaking, here, of solar winds, spikes, or emissions. We speak of huge swaths of plasma simply disappearing from your star's corporeal form.

Do you want to know what this transition looks like? You have it available to you, from what we can confirm is a relatively reliable photographic record that shows you images of the sun, where colossal bands of its fiery form are simply "missing" one day, and back the next.

You, yourselves, are experiencing these moments of slipping out of 3D and into the otherworldly four-dimensional reference point where you experience timelessness and telepathic mind linkage. Confused and unsure, you then pop back into the three-dimensional theater of your known reality, which is no less an illusion than that which you experienced in that brief encounter with the fourth! Clutching your handle on time and place—markers that provide a sense of security—you consternate over what you just witnessed, with concern that you may really be "slipping" mentally.

Some of these moments you are already well aware of; some, you are not, for they can be mere nanoseconds on your mind screen—and it is only natural that you are left to question: "What just happened?" "Am I imagining this?"

These increasingly occurring events of the multidimensional kind are teaching you, through the conscious and subconscious layers of your intellect, knowledge, and experience, what subtle energies are escalating, what others are duly waning and letting go, and how all these changes and energy shifts will carry you through the greatest astral journey of all your lifetimes: stellar ascension.

If you could see as we see, where the physical universe is a tiny fraction of all that is available to the telescopically telepathic observer, you would be utterly awestruck by the accelerated pace of so many worlds in evolution, and the beauteousness of all that is manifesting throughout your solar space.

Knowing what you now know about the effect of consciousness upon water, for one example, and how every molecule reflects the soul's intention to coalesce in sacred design, can you fathom what that looks like, across the entire solar system, in terms of color, rhythm, and geometric artistry? Every planet has its vibratory signature, its musical chord, and its essential underpinnings, reflecting, in due course, the consciousness of beings that reside there. No words can define it . . . for how can one explain Creator?

How can mere words communicate the infinite palette of godly design?

You are witness to this spectacular array of Creation everywhere in nature—where it has not been artificially redesigned by human hand. Imagine, if you can, how that appears in a galactic sense, as we specifically intend as the embodiment of your solar family: the sun, planets, moons, icy shields, asteroids, and the dust of souls and atoms, in transit.

If only we could open an observation window, for you, that could shrink space to a manageable enough quantum, we would be enabled to demonstrate how change is manifesting upon worlds beyond yours: places where frozen oceans of solid ice have begun to flow; worlds where once furious landscapes now yield to the gentle breeze; others where cold darkness is being filled with the warmth of life-enhancing, glorious light.

We can give you our perspectives, but we cannot give you our "eyes." For even if we could, what of wonder?

Your dreams of what will come . . . your hope, empowered with the clearest intentions—these are the magician's wands of your own magical journey. Nothing can ever supplant personal experience, nor be more beautiful and extraordinary than your own divine visions and their creations.

From the looks of things on Planet Earth, you surely sense that you are teetering on some sort of cataclysmic pinnacle, and that the slowly climbing rollercoaster cart that got you there is about to take you careening down the track, in irreversible forward motion. Whether you await that passage in glorious anticipation of the thrill of all that will follow, or whether you cower in dread, refusing to look ahead, remember: you signed up for that ride at the soul level—consciously and without reservation. You got a glimpse of its gigantic frame, towering, mighty, and electrifying, lording over the horizon of a future physical life—your current lifetime (or more specifically, one of the many you are living simultaneously)—and you made the very conscious decision to climb aboard . . . to experience how it would feel, and where it would take you.

And "where it has taken you" is to one of the most extraordinary events ever to occur in the universe of matter: the ascension of a star . . . your sun.

You knew it, you signed up for it, and here you are.

Understanding that the universe is in perpetual motion, and that all existence experiences itself in various states of birth, growth, death, rebirth, and progression, we are particularly intrigued to see how your central star, Ra, is accelerating, at this point in space-time. The quickening of your entire solar system is causing a vibratory shift that is far more accelerated than the outer environment that surrounds the entire solar sheath.

This is quite fascinating. You have moved into an area of your galaxy that is highly charged, but it cannot keep pace with your sun. Think that through for a moment.

Can you fathom the enormity of the sun's escalation? Remember, too, that all the planetary beings, within the solar family, are subject to and are a reflection of those energies . . . and you get a hint of what is the "knockdown effect" across the planetary expanse for all life, at every station, and in every imaginable and unimaginable form. It is a celestial extravaganza we are witnessing here, as are other watchers from around the multiverse, and it is something quite spectacular.

So intense is the immense galactic shift, around and within your solar body, that we feel compelled to describe everything in your sun's environment as racing completely out of control, in the highest sense of that expressed terminology. And "out of control" is where you, the awakening, strive to be, for your own planet and your entire civilization. Ironically, in order to be finally freed of the controls upon your civilization, you must first bear witness to a global society that appears to be off the rails, in a state of orchestrated, almost maniacal chaos.

Despite the appearance of all that is inharmonious and anarchic in your immediate line of vision, or that is threatening to be, down new or unfamiliar roads, always remember that this is your impetus. Change itself is the trigger that incites the difficult process of liberation. You are pushing through your fear of the tyrants and thieves who have dominated human social evolution for so many millennia, imposing their misguided will upon the collective consciousness of all human beings—even upon the Earth herself.

Eager to move forward, you are pushing through the final stages of your desperate struggle against the tenacious grip of those controllers, in order to reach true freedom of mind, body, and soul. And you are well on your way to achieving that goal—for, as we told you time ago, their grip is weakening—and so, their hold over you.

Your sun is the engine that is propelling Earth through these difficult times, when your world seems upside down, where good appears to be bad, right appears to be wrong, and darkness pretends to be light, cloaked in mystery. Think of that, anytime you despair for the future of your planet.

Earth is one car on a cosmic train, and nothing can stop the momentum of that galactic convoy. You have been programmed to think of yourself lost in space, in so many ways, but you are not. You are in the passenger's seat, riding the Great Interstellar Express, pulling out of New York Central.

Still, you feel these Desert Days upon the Earth, where everything is in a state of revolutionary upheaval, because, from the point of view of your civilization, the overturning of all that has bound you has you tilting, just like the axis of your planet. But you **are** coming to the end of this phase and you can feel it—because you know that the pitch of human disharmony is absolutely unsustainable.

It must resolve. And it will.

You are desperate to know when . . . and to be assured that you are headed to lighter ground. We hear your implorations for help from beyond; we hear your questions and pleas. They demand very specific answers, and precision time lines about events so galactic in scope, so essential to your personal soul experience and the free will of your sun, that they defy any and all explanation.

What you want, very clearly, is a time line on the no-time.

That is an utter contradiction . . . one that we cannot resolve for you.

Your sun, Ra, determines the time; it is the key player in your evolution. It decides when it is ready, and it sets the metronome for all that follows. We can read the vibrational shifts, the alterations of form, and the waves they stir on the space-time continuum, but we cannot tell you, with any specificity, when your sun will take that giant leap: from those illusory bands into the fourth dimension.

Then, there is the greater philosophical and moral issue at stake, one that we cannot ignore. What would it matter if you knew the date and time (both illusions of the third dimension) of your full emergence into the fourth dimension—where there is no time? How would that knowledge affect the right now of your life or, more specifically, the free will that drives your every discovery and moves you forward? Would you surrender to the inevitability of that passage, no longer standing for the Earth, or for all the good works that you are doing to raise the pitch of human experience . . . and no longer serving as the lightworkers of your communities?

Do you see how that information—a prophetic date and time that could alter your present course—would disable you, in so many ways . . . ways that are not in your best interest, nor that of the entirety? That is the very last thing we wish for you and, when you think it through, you know it is not what you wish for yourselves.

Your good deeds, your higher thoughts, and the love that pour into the ethos of Gaia, with the express intention of healing the disharmonies that abound there, are all part and process of what you came into this lifetime to contribute and to make yours forever.

Lightworkers, spirit warriors, starseed children—hear the call.

Your vigilance now, and your determination to hold the planet in your love, are the keys to unlocking the kingdom. We believe that it is the unknown that is the wonder, and that it is the journey that leads you to an illusive destination one thinks of as "there" that is by far more extraordinary than anything that might even remotely resemble "being there." Do you agree with us that this quest is within you, within us all . . . and that all conscious beings, sparks of divine consciousness, possess utopia in their souls?

If you can grasp and honor that the goal is within us all, then surely you are willing to let go of all that which resembles your own need for control over any given experience, time, emotion—and to simply ride it out, celebrating the experience, paying attention to every living thing around you.

"Yes, yes," we hear you reply. "That is all well and good. But when will I finally achieve ascension? When?"

Children of Gaia, what we can tell you with absolute certainty is that Ra's current mutations are unparalleled in form and manifestation, so much so that your star is becoming increasingly unrecognizable. Certainly, it is behaving in ways that it never has before now—ask any noncommissioned astrophysicist! These erratic and scientifically inexplicable solar mutations have nothing to do with the star's cyclical history of solar peaks and valleys, which have your sun's energies ranging from silent and brooding in one minute, to raging and explosive in the next—energies from its fiery wands pounding into the shields of every planet and moon in its wake.

No, what you are witnessing now, in the gaseous plasma of your central star, is not about cycles of solar activity, and it cannot be categorized or explained away in those terms. What is happening now, without question, is the sun's perpetual and advancing transmutation, from one dimensional vibration to the next: reshaping, remolding, and refining its vibratory signature as a physical mass, to one of a more subtle expression.

If you really think about it, and if you observe the images available to you from your space agencies and independent astronomers, it does make total sense. In fact, we humbly submit that it is the only explanation that does!

Like some great celestial magic act, it appears that huge areas of the sun keep disappearing completely, as if the center of your universe were breaking down, coming apart at the seams. In actuality, what is happening is that portions of your star are quickening faster than others, which of course is understandable—for in the world of matter and form, this fiery mass is not one dimensional, of a uniform consistency. It exists as an enormous spectrum, ranging in luminosity, temperature, density, and all manner of measures. Because of that diversity, some areas of the solar field are vibrating much more rapidly, and these mammoth swaths of plasma are reaching resonance with the fourth density, momentarily slipping into that dimension. However, because the entirety of the solar mass is still unable to hold resonance in that more subtle density of the fourth, those gaseous tongues of solar energy reassemble back into the plasma mass that is still present in physical form, over and over again.

This will continue to occur and to reoccur until resonance with the fourth dimension has been achieved across the board, on every level. At that point, the star soars through its own astral cord, and moves on!

Select images of the sun's phenomena are available, we remind you, as a photographic record, for there is great interest, it goes without saying, from your government. We recommend that you study them with more than just passing interest, for, even if you do grasp the enormity of solar ascension, and its meaning for all of your lives, it is still amazing to see it happening, recorded for your visual interpretations. If, instead, you still question the idea of how your sun has begun its ascension, or if it is simply beyond your ability to comprehend how it will manifest, then see for yourself.

The disappearing act on your sun's surface simply cannot be accounted for, in any existing scientific terminology; if anything, it negates the pre-existing notions regarding its mass, emissions, and electromagnetic force fields. It simply does not fit any preconceived notion of a star's structure or behavior.

It does not fit the third dimension.

No existing data defining the sun's magnetic shifts, its radioactive dynamics, or any other scientific measure can explain what is occurring in the sun or any one of the planets, keeping your conventional scientists in a state of significant confusion. They do not understand spirit; they cannot understand ascension of the soul of any being, no matter how minute, no matter how vast and immeasurable.

As for the skeptics (for, no doubt, you encounter so many in your lives): ask them how they can explain away thirty percent of the sun's mass disappearing in one minute, and reappearing in another. How is it possible to see through holes that have formed in the sun's immense body? Ask them—have they even seen these images? Let the conventional thinkers explain them away . . .

From our viewing stations of the physical plane, we can actually observe how this "plasma" slips into the fourth density, where its consistency, luminosity, and electromagnetism spectrums still appear very much the same as they did in the physical. But again, it is pulled back to the physical, tethered between the two dimensions. It cannot hold resonance in the fourth—at least not yet. However, as you see holes in the sun over and over again, you realize that, in the context of an imminent point in time, it is soon to make that leap a permanent one.

From blinking in and out of the fourth dimension, as you have begun to do, to merging, definitively, into the fourth, your sun, and all the living beings upon other planetary worlds in the neighborhood of your solar system, are in position, ready to go!

Since our first transmissions through this channel, until this moment, two decades hence, we have given you space and time to assimilate all that has transpired, passing through your earthly time of 2012, when the Great Wheel or "Great Shift of Ages," and your planet's own axis, turned.

It has not reversed entirely, but Gaia's axial tilt has most definitely shifted.

From icy terrains near the northern pole, to snow-covered beaches of the southern hemisphere, and everywhere in between—native wisdom keepers of your planet are doing what they can to awaken humanity to this pressing reality. They are still so close to the earth, the sea, and the sky, and by nature of that closeness, so connected to the spirit of Gaia, that they can feel those wheels turning.

They know the sun is rising from a different horizon than it did before your year 2012; they know the seasons, the natural sequences of the Earth, because they are attuned to the soul of the Great Mother. Moreover, they feel her heart, expressed in the harmonies of nature: energies, they are telling you, that are waning; life, they are showing you, that is disappearing from the face of the Earth. We submit that their profound observations are no less accurate than the measures of any technological equipment currently defining your celestial position in relationship to the sun, and the great cosmic changes that affect it.

We hear the debate raging amongst you, for many are still in denial of extreme earth changes, and for reasons that surely are clear to you, the whole question of climate and geophysical changes on your planet remains something akin to a sociopolitical football game—where there can be no winner. It provokes division between different poles of observation, where instead you, the greater human race, would glean so much important insight if only your opposing teams would join forces, center field, to redirect those energies for the healing of Gaia.

We are not interested in becoming embroiled in the system of justification and accusation with regard to such information, and the gathering, or not, of significant data to prove the obvious. That is, and will always be, a lesson in futility. What needs to be addressed is that, despite artificially induced weather patterns, something is warming your planet. Is it the sun, or is it human negligence?

We submit that it is both.

You do know that it is in the interest of corporations that exploit the Earth that you continue to burn fossil fuels for energy, effectively blocking the development and advancement of forward-thinking technologies that utilize alternative sources—clean energy—capable of serving the energy needs of the entire planet. Suffice to say that all integrated, peaceful civilizations draw energy directly from their own central star, or from a collective of stellar bodies within their reach.

You do surely understand that denying humankind's contribution to the warming of your planet weakens your resolve. It stalls any and all legitimate attempts to put an end to that highly profitable, absolutely destructive solution to your energy needs.

You are witness to the enormous alterations of weather patterns and their ensuing disruption, through droughts, floods, and all manner of disasters. There are also geological markers that indicate shifts in the very ground you walk upon. They are fierce, they are more and more frequent, and they are changing the landscape of your cities and villages forever.

Anytime you have such intense earthquakes, as those that have been occurring now, surrounding the turning of the cosmic Wheel of Ages, you are going to see the balance, in this case the actual axis of the planet, altered. Several factors are affecting Earth's stability and geophysical deterioration, and we do confirm that, despite human alteration of your weather systems, and of the auric field or atmospheric layers that surround the planet, there is an unprecedented solar effect contributing very significantly to those changes.

All the planets in your sun system are mutating form, energy fields, luminosity, and magnetism. Earth is one of the most extreme of all concerned, but there is plenty more taking place in your neighborhood in space: upon the planets and moons and asteroids, yes, but certainly not limited to them. The actual space between them, and how they adhere, as we mentioned earlier, is changing dramatically . . . and that is clearly the sun's doing.

In the case of your solar family, what happens to one celestial form happens, in some degree, to all—so you must be curious to know how things are unfolding on other planets. The sensitives amongst you feel the sway of the planets, the sun, and the moon so powerfully, and you have honored their forces and energies for centuries, throughout so many traditions . . . so many rituals. Your moon, pulling the tides, shifting your emotions, is example enough for you to know how important every single celestial being is to your own process, and to the communal behavior and perception. You have only to study the local news, to chart the increase in violent behaviors, when the moon is full, wreaking havoc on the emotional waters of the emotionally unstable. Similarly, and, following the example of those interactive planetary energies, you understand, at the deepest levels, that what happens to one of you happens to all, on varying levels, and in varying degrees.

It is what you do with those energies that makes each experience so extraordinarily unique to you, as an individual observer and participant—experience, you well know, that you bring to the collective pool of energy and awareness. We ask that you bear this in mind as we describe, from our observations, the most significant shifts that can be observed within your entire star system, all orchestrated by your star's own mutations, the charged galactic environment surrounding it, and the field of interstellar activity of the "interdependent energy body" of your solar field.

We wish to focus primarily upon your star, and your family of planets, moons, and asteroids, but we shall go on to speak of quite the dramatic increase in waves of space dust permeating your celestial fields.

Your solar system is creating quite a musical stir at this hour of its immense transition. It is an intense, high-pitched frequency, the accelerated whir of cosmic bodies in highly agitated space . . . and beings from many layers, or densities (as we prefer to describe them), are particularly focused upon Gaia. They are concerned over how she is struggling to push through the disharmonies of her entire planetary expanse, as she accelerates, along with the other planets, moons, and asteroids—even the interstellar dust—that comprise your solar family.

All life there—on every single planet—is, by nature of that acceleration, shifting dramatically . . . as are you. It is so very important, now more than ever before, that you understand and embrace the idea that you are not alone in this process. Dramatic change is under way, upon every single planet in your system, on every moon, every asteroid, and every orb.

From the subatomic level, to the primary elements of matter, to the alteration of form and its effect on the interactive life forms of any given environment, everything is rapidly evolving now, in line with your sun's own emissions, transmutations, and song.

The closest comparison we can make to the human experience is that moment when the body is about to experience a "kundalini rising." Like the chakric wheels that run your own electromagnetic bodies and energy fields, all celestial beings that comprise the body of your solar system are attuning to these higher frequencies. Each planet and every living being upon it, in kind, knows this music, for it is the quintessential "soul music" of the Cosmos. And even if, in your star system, it has never before reached such a crescendo, each living being and every planetary deity still experiences the intensity, as an extension of its own essence, and responds, each in its own way, in an immense quickening.

You can be certain that scientists from around your world are studying the shifting energies of all the planetary bodies in orbit around your sun, with great concern, for only the secret government knows the big picture. These are agents that have several levels of security clearance above presidents and the visible political players who appear to represent governments. At the very top are the Annunaki overlords—you know them as the reptilian aristocracy. It is they who have been so busy lowering Earth's frequencies to the lowest possible denominator, attempting to pull Nebiru through the ascension.

Why do you think they have spent so much effort to block your view of the sun, through the use of chemically induced cloud formations? They cannot bear to see the light that is rising, foiling their master plan—and they do not want you to see it, either.

They are in the throes of the final scene of their long drama in the earth realm, and they realize how they are the cause of their own destruction. As for you—your fate is insignificant to them, for they do not care about the planet. They never have.

They do not care about you, whatsoever.

Despite the chaos of this last show of force, they have finally realized that Nebiru will not be saved—it never could have been. To reach resonance with that planet, Earth would have to have been almost completely destroyed—and they have taken the planet close, you recognize that, but their plan has backfired. In the light of the unstoppable new age upon you, they are seeing themselves disintegrate, like salt on a lizard's tail.

Their suppression is causing you to rise above them, more and more—every day. The sun and the Earth are unstoppable fountains of higher energies that are counteracting the drone of their intent with a chorus of higher octaves, sweeter songs, and music from the soul of Gaia.

And so, their dream is over; their motivation is gone—and they want to hate you for their own misguided programs and failed dreams. They loathe failure and they want to blame you—the uncontrollable ones—who refuse to bow down and yield your power. To you they wish to leave a disenfranchised planet that has failed to perform to their needs, so they do not want it to perform to yours—for that would mean total humiliation, and defeat.

Warriors to the bitter end, they cannot bear it.

The scientific, aerospace community is still unaware of what is actually occurring, because they still do not believe in ascension, nor do they understand it. But they are very concerned about what they are witnessing in space. An unprecedented number of satellites is being disabled, both on the planet's surface and in the outer atmosphere. This transmutation of energy and form is even altering the space junk and technological shields in place around your globe. They admit to being baffled, because, as always, their laws of physics are being made redundant.

They see the sun, which they have conceptualized, by its material manifestations, to be plasma of gases and radioactive combustion. And yet, its properties, and those extreme and perpetual alterations, break all the rules of established science. Despite all their technological advancements, there is still no equipment available that adequately measures or predicts the sun's emissions, flares, and now this—its partial disappearance!

Most importantly, they do not understand the consciousness of the sun, nor any star, for that matter. In truth, science barely allows for consciousness to play any role, anywhere life exists. Until they recognize that the sun is a conscious being, with a very specific purpose, they can only remain bewildered as to the cause and effect of the sun's mutation, particularly those mysterious coronal holes, which are precursors to its complete dematerialization.

As we have stated, there exists no technology, no data analysis, nor methodology to measure soul and the progression of spirit. More importantly, one would have to believe that the soul exists at all, before setting out to measure its wisdom, its force, and its sovereign direction. Only a comprehensive science that, at the very least, considers the soul—its creative will and existential purpose—can ever begin to understand the celestial dynamics of ascension.

Hence, we remind you that what comes from the scientists is limited to the observation of events, or manifestations upon the sun's surface, and the sun's effect upon the planets held in orbit around it. That observation, of itself, alters the expression of those events. What is happening at the soul level, which is the core issue of ascension . . . that eludes science, completely.

Hopefully, this will change. In the meantime, let the immensity of that process be felt by all beings, not only those who are awakening enough to feel the soul of the sun, the Earth, and the stars, lighting up their spirit, deep inside: spirit that cannot be dissected, measured, or extinguished.

Then, there is the music—the celestial symphony that cannot be heard through your physical ears, for, despite the broad range of levels, they are not attuned to celestial sounds. Some animals, of course, hear beyond your range, for the express purpose of their locomotion and survival in their ecosystems: from the tiny moth, to the mighty elephant and Great Whales, and countless other species in between. But, when you are fluttering in and out of the fourth dimension, or in spirit, soaring beyond your physical form in dreams or astral journeys, you are capable of hearing the song of the universe.

What is important here is that you understand that you will begin, if you have not already, to perceive the rhythm, the hum, and the chorus of all the planets—and this, as we have referred to before, is the Music of the Spheres. In the divine ratio of celestial beings that cling to your sun, orbiting endlessly around that flame, there exists a higher form of music that is the harmonic resonance of consciousness, playing its soul into the cosmic medium. These extraordinary tones and spherical vibrations always reflect the positions of the planets, in relationship to each other, and to the sun— and, no doubt, to stars beyond your solar body. However, for our purposes here, let us measure, as best we can, the imprint of celestial music upon the immediate environment: from the "core" of your central sun, out into the auric sheath of the entire system.

We know that the term and the concept of the "Music of the Spheres" are not new to you, for the ancient wisdom keepers spoke of it. The one, Pythagoras, could hear it playing in his mind, which made staying anchored in the third dimension no easy feat. He could manage it for short intervals of time. A star walker of the highest integrity, he tried as much as was possible, in his day, to share the knowledge of the Cosmos of Soul through his mystery school, but only a select few were prepared to recognize the truth of those teachings. Not even the High Priests of Egypt could grasp his knowledge, for they were too steeped in their own traditions to recognize the genius of a "mere mortal." Little did they know that he was a god, in their terms, for, as the greatest time traveler to ever walk the Earth, he was present in every pivotal moment when civilization was spiking to new heights of acquired knowledge and collective consciousness. He walked as Hermes Trismegistus, Thoth, and Imhotep, in and out, skating across the space-time continuum just as eloquently as he navigated the higher dimensions—and still does.

When you start hearing the Music of the Spheres, you will see him, somewhere between and beyond the violet and magenta hues of the rainbow.

Now, if you consider that your reality is merely a demonstration of sound, and light frequencies, interacting, and that there is far more beyond your range of perception than there is within it, you may be freed from any preconceived notion of what is real, or not. You may then be more able to recognize how the sun's accelerating vibrations are changing the pitch of the entire system, and how all the planets, in turn, are playing to the Maestro.

Earth's electromagnetic resonance has changed—and so has her music. This acceleration plays through all of her fields, all life forms: the crystalline matrix, the molten lava, waters, air—and the DNA lattice that underlies all biology upon and within the planetary being. Attuned to the new harmonics of an awakening star, the earth song plays through the atmospheric levels of the auric field, and plays that crescendo, as orchestrated by the sun, coursing through space.

As it traverses the galactic field held by your sun, so does it activate and agitate (in a very positive sense) the subatomic realm that is the foundation of all that exists. We are telling you that your sun and your Earth, and all the other planets, are in concert, playing the vibrations of your solar acceleration, into the very DNA of your being—and that can only mean, in a very beautiful sense, that you are being rewired for sound! The music changes all the time, but it always reflects divine proportion, rhythm, and pitch.

We have spoken at length of the DNA, and how the dormant strands are beginning to reassemble into geometric forms that represent sacred expansions upon the basic tetrahedron—forms that are restructuring and self-replicating within your double helix. We mention it here, as it pertains to the music we have described emanating from your star, across the solar body, and into the cloud, or aura, that surrounds it.

If the galactic space surrounding this immense solar field is still not vibrating as quickly as the sun, well . . . perhaps it has still not integrated the new octaves.

But it will . . . as will you—right down to the DNA light strings of your subatomic essence: the microverse.

12

Electromagnetism
The Glue That Binds

Come aboard our solar exploration vessel—stirring the wonder of your creative imagination into the cosmic cup of spinning celestial worlds—and join us, as we observe current and developing advancements within your sun's own body, across the interstellar plains, and upon those planets that we find to be of particular interest, insofar as their bodies and energy fields are manifesting the most noteworthy alterations of form and electromagnetic emanations.

There is a significant quickening, brightening, and altering of all these celestial forms, which can be observed more clearly now, thanks to advancements in your space exploration and satellite probes. You will soon be hearing of several newly discovered planets in your solar system. They are tiny, compared to even some planetary moons, but there are also life forms on those dwarfs.

Because the sun's energies wax and wane as cyclical manifestations, which seem to correspond to an approximate eleven-year time frame (always calculating time in terms of earth measurement), one can debate whether the activation of the planets in your solar system, and of the life forms that they bear, is solely due to surges in the sun's electromagnetic fields. We submit that what is manifest in this final preparatory phase of solar ascension is not only the sun's own surging energy and physical transmutation—in and out of "form." There is also acceleration in the highly charged galactic environment in which your star finds itself at this very critical juncture. It may not be as intense as that of your sun, as we previously mentioned, but it is increasing, proportionally. It is no accident that the positively galvanized galactic space of highly charged photonic activity will serve to host your sun's passage, like some incredibly designed birthing station, from where you will be launched to the fourth density.

In this divine dance of interactive, conscious beings (giants, to you, relative to your own form and energetic potentialities), mutation of form and refinement of energy occur not only from the sun—out to its orbiting planets and their moons. We are simply pointing out, for the sake of precision, that these changes also occur in the highly charged space around the sun, activating the auric sheath that surrounds the solar system. That, in turn, plays its active part in stimulating every particle, from dust to aster-oid—in synthesis with the sun's own imprint, and as a reflection of the soul of the Cosmos.

From the most remote planets in the sun's body—and out into the cloud[12] that surrounds it, everything is speeding up . . . and everything is heating up. Like a macrocosmic representation of your own auric field, the "cloud" we speak of is your star's auric barrier, a protective womb-like shield, which also echoes the health of the entire system. It is in a state of expansion.

All conscious beings create an auric field, reflecting and supporting their biological, physical, and spiritual energy bodies. Earth, representative of all planetary beings, is surrounded by such an aura, comprised of many layers, which some describe as its "atmosphere," and others as its "aura," determined by the context in which it is being described and the observer's understanding of spirit. Despite scientific claims to the contrary, all planets have auric fields and hence, no matter how imperceptible, they all have some form of atmosphere.

These atmospheric layers are of extreme interest to your space inves-tigators, for they are a reflection of a planet's health and its constitution, which is almost always negatively affected by its technological and mili-tary prowess.

We have spoken to you of devices and activities being utilized by your military to manipulate Earth's shield—particularly, but not limited to, the ionosphere. This is creating disturbance in the magnetosphere, the outer layer of the planet's auric field, which is dominated by its magnetic force field, in direct line to interact with the sun's erratic and unpredictable electromagnetic activity: electric and magnetic properties . . . two com-plementary aspects of the same energetic force. This is so important to your understanding of how the sun pushes and pulls at the Earth, and how it will draw all of the planets through its astral cord, at the appropriate moment.

---

[12]   Known in scientific terms as the "oort cloud": http://space-facts.com/oort-cloud/

All planets exhibit magnetism through their atmospheric outer bodies, which are complex in nature and form; but, for the sake of clarity, we agree to focus upon the magnetosphere—the outer sheath. This layer protects the planet from direct bombardment by solar winds and high-energy particles, by deflecting them from the direct point of impact, and then spreading them around the entirety of the planet. In essence, the magnetosphere distributes cosmic solar rays over the body of the planet, and then directs them back out into interstellar space.

Here we will contradict your scientists, by declaring that all planets with atmospheres exhibit properties and manifestations of this layer—the magnetosphere barrier. They say this is not so. However, it is our observation that even the most remote planet from the sun still requires a system that will distribute the sun's electromagnetic emanations around its globe, so necessary to the stability and balance of the celestial form . . . and to any and all life that it supports. As you race toward deep space exploration, your astrophysicists will finally concur that this is an aspect inherent in the auric fields of all planetary bodies.

Some planets exhibit relatively weak magnetospheres, such as that of Mars; some are stronger . . . the strongest being that which surrounds Jupiter.

It is a complex interaction, whose science is not necessary to our purpose here, and which, no doubt, is off-putting to you on some levels— for the complexities of galactic physics are often difficult to engage with. However, as it is our intent to describe the relationship of planet to planet, and planet to sun, we do need to touch upon the celestial mechanics in play.

What matters is that you grasp a very basic concept, with regard to the interplanetary/interstellar magnetic field. It is an interdependent, interactive system and it exists across the board, in various degrees, from the inner planets to those in remote positions from the sun.

Like all celestial bodies, and similar to your own human form, the sun is an electromagnetic organism, displaying electric currents and magnetic properties, determined by factors that have to do with the proper functioning of its corporeal structure, its interactive relationship to the galactic field, and its conscious energy requirements. Moons, even aster-oids (described to you as gigantic rocks in space), can exhibit magnetic fields, for they possess the essential mineral components—nickel, iron, and other minerals—and can be magnetized by neighboring planets.

So, you have a solar system comprised of a central sun, planets, moons, asteroids, interstellar dust, and significant debris, all connected by the electromagnetic properties of the star: solar flares and electric emanations that reach even the farthest planets out from the central star. What we find most extraordinary, and what we wish to have you contemplate, is how these celestial bodies are bound to the sun in perfect proportions, like chords on a piano.

The distance between planets and their moons, the position of these celestial bodies in their orbital paths, and the energetic fields of their inner and outer bodies will all be in perfect alignment—exhibiting sacred cosmometry—when your star pulls everything through its ascension cord, and all emerge in the new light of the fourth dimension.

Let us examine the most significant developments in your solar family, expressions of planetary refinement for ascension.

Earth

With regard to your planet of choice, the lower levels of the magneto-sphere overlap with the layer known as the "ionosphere." This is why we have warned you of the effects of human interference with the ionosphere, not only on the planet itself, but also throughout its protective shields. When you cook the ionosphere, causing highly energized protons and electrons to heat, you are disturbing the magnetosphere . . . and that is a very dangerous thing to do.

Earth's magnetic fields are reversing, the axis has shifted its tilt, and the magnetic pole known to you as the northern pole is drifting east. You need not attach any fear whatsoever to this information, nor to your sense of its significance, for this is a natural evolutionary process for the planet. It is not the apocalyptic scenario, painted for you by mind terrorists who wish to keep you in fear. This is a gradual process; it is a relationship dynamic, sun to planet, and it is a precursor to the ascension journey.

That is not to say that there will be no adverse manifestations from these galactic movements, for you are already witness to cataclysmic events in the geophysical formations of the planet. Always bearing in mind that Gaia is a living being, you are going to feel and experience significant shifts in her physical, emotional, and mental bodies. Volcanoes are erupting; earthquakes (natural and provoked) are shaking the ground you walk on; clear water glaciers are breaking away into the salty ocean seas. The very crust of the planet is sinking, pulling apart at the seams.

Understandably these are often tragic events, for your civilization's needs have pushed humanity to the extreme regions of the globe, and Gaia has no place left to release pent-up energies without causing devastation to human life. We invite you to observe these phenomena with due circumspection, always remembering that the planet needs room to breathe—to stretch, shift, and dance to the cosmic beat.

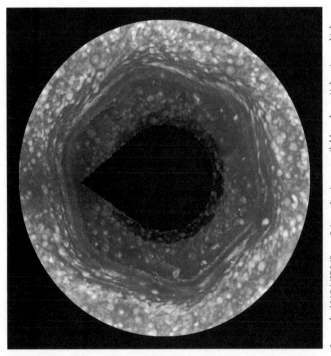

Image by NASA/JPL/Space Science Institute; available at https://photojournal.jpl .nasa.gov/catalog/PIA11682

Saturn

No discussion of Saturn would be complete without acknowledging the perfect hexagonal cloud cover that shrouds a perpetual storm at its northern pole, extending far into the planet's inner atmosphere. Your astrophysicists search for answers to what could cause such a precise formation, but, as is increasingly the case—they remain "baffled." The appearance of this geometric form, in the atmosphere of a nearby planet, doesn't fit any decipherable physical laws. In fact, nothing about it makes sense—and it never will, until they recognize that sacred form is the nature of all things in the multiverse. It is, as we have so often shown you, the underpinning of the great design behind all of Creation.

This hexagonal mystery reflects the planet's conscious expression of the Hermetic wisdom inherent within the six-sided star: "As above, so below; and as below, so above."

As if that were not enough to titillate your imagination, what is quite extraordinary is that this pole has suddenly changed color—from blue, to a golden hue. What more of a statement could one make than that, to describe a planet in the process of accelerated refinement?

Those enigmatic rings that surround Saturn, considered emblematic of the dust and gases that once surrounded the sun, are actually narrowing significantly, and will soon vanish altogether. The particle density that forms their structure is much reduced, and again, that has everything to do with the planet's shift to a more refined density and higher vibration. It is our observation that the tiny moons that appear inside those layers are being absorbed into the planet's material plane and possibly will disappear, starting with those closest to its surface.

Jupiter

The year 2012 impacted the giant, Jupiter, with meteorite bombardment so immense in scope that even amateur earth astronomers were able to observe it. Since then, the planet's atmosphere has changed its range of colors on the visible spectrum, but also in the invisible, or infrared, range.

Like Saturn's disappearing rings, gaseous bands in Jupiter's southern sphere have disappeared, signs that its auric field is responding to heightened solar activity and the weakening of its magnetic field. All of this, of course, is in preparation for its journey through the sun's astral cord and onto the higher vibratory fields of four-dimensional density.

Mars

Your not-so-distant neighbor is in the process of regaining its life-sustaining atmosphere, largely due to your government's terraforming project there, in collaboration with (and under strict surveillance from) its Martian partners. The "free" energy, being suppressed or denied you on Earth, is the source utilized to create this effect. It is directed solar power that allows for the melting of the polar caps, which, in turn, is releasing high levels of carbon dioxide—and the chain reaction unfolds. You know, from the so-named "greenhouse effect" of such gases on Earth, that this generates heat: the heat needed to warm and strengthen the fledgling atmosphere there.

The technicians of the Martian underground—human and alien alike—have successfully catapulted this accelerated greenhouse effect that has the ice poles melting significantly on that planet, and water flowing again. They are successfully restoring forests there, and introducing new species of flora to the planet—thanks also to the contribution of seeds from Earth. Those so-called seed banks that have been buried under the ice and earth on your planet provide ample varieties to regenerate Mars completely, and it has been very successful. Those gardens are growing and, so, the oxygen.

The electromagnetic field surrounding Mars has been so very weak until now—subject to solar waves that strip the atmosphere. But this too is changing. Soon you will be made aware that Mars has regained its atmosphere and that, contrary to the stark images you are shown, it is host to oceans, rivers, and verdant regions—and, lest we forget, to an existent subsurface civilization that has begun to rise above the confines of its inner world.

Pluto

Speaking of atmospheres and their galactic functions and manifestations, consider the minute planet, the farthest out, which is so distant from your sun that it is almost impossible to imagine that it can survive at all—much less to consider biological life there. The existence of life on Pluto is no less remarkable, really, than your discovery of aquatic life in the deepest trenches of your oceans, so far from light and the warmth of the sun that, based on an understanding of biology, it makes no sense that life can exist there at all. And, yet, life proliferates even there. Some beings have sensors that serve as radar through the darkness, and others with their own built-in electric lighting illuminate the way as they go.

This is the case on that distant planet.

There, in the icy cold of the outer solar body, this dwarf is also heating up. In fact, its rate of acceleration is far greater than that of the other planets, including your own. From a strictly galactic point of view, it is being facilitated by high-energy streams surrounding the entire body of the solar system, compensating for weaker solar support.

The Sun

Let us reexamine the sun itself, for it is in an absolute frenzy on many levels: mutating form, as it alters its consistency and changes density regularly—to such a point that it actually partially disappears. The sun's mutations and its progressively intensified solar winds seem to provide no clear explanation of just what is happening, or the true nature of its composition and form, for increasingly worried scientific communities on Earth. Your conscious, living sun is mutating as part of this process of refinement, transmuting its own matter (and that of all celestial material within its being) to a less dense manifestation, as a very conscious and self-aware process of its spiritual exaltation.

Some of its form, this gaseous energy that simply disappears and then inexplicably reappears, is already experiencing itself in the fourth, fifth, and sixth dimensions—as the energy rises, and then wanes—still not entirely prepared for its transition . . . still unable to establish resonance at those higher frequencies. It then slips back into the 3D matrix, and reappears in its gaseous form, temporarily filling the "holes" observed in your telescopes. With each energy burst, returning that partial body to the third dimension becomes more chaotic, as if unlearning the matrix of its 3D consistency: the form and the shape it has held in the physical universe. This explains why you are witness to moments when there is an absolute hole in the center or around the outer regions of your sun—and why in another moment it is not there.

It may be difficult for the logical mind to embrace this concept, but we assure you that this is the way things are unfolding in your solar field. Again, as always, we invite you to scrutinize the information we share with you and accept what rings as truth in your hearts, reflecting back to you your own deeply rooted understanding of all things—from the microcosmic nature of your atomic essence, to your contemplations as starseed dust of the multiverse.

Whatever does not resonate as truth, discard. Or perhaps, better yet, let it sit somewhere in the corner of your mind, where possible realities can be explored when and if you are ready to go there.

Referring again to the sun and its partial disappearing act, we remind you that, similarly, you, and all the beings of your planet, are blinking into the fourth dimension now and then, getting glimpses of other realities, and then slipping back into the third. For some, this is an illustrious, light-filled adventure of discovery; for others, it is a frightening sense of losing one's grip on reality.

Either way, you are having quite a time trying to understand what is happening, and even more difficulty trying to put a name to it. Is time slipping? Are you becoming more psychic, more attuned to other realms? When do you arrive at the point where light surrounds you, when the drama of suffering has been supplanted by compassion, love, and beauty? Is it possible, truly possible, that you are already experiencing the fourth dimension, but simply cannot yet identify it as such?

Yes. The answer is that all of this is happening. And it is going to accelerate now, in these next pivotal earth years, so hold on.

You are in for the ride of your (many) lifetimes.

13

Starseed

The Soul of Interstellar Dust

Your galactic explorers, and by that we mean those who are observing and photographing space (whether by satellite probes, telescopic devices, or merely through windows of vessels in space), are seeing an inordinate increase in particles within your solar system, which they refer to as "interstellar dust." Astrophysicists explain this plankton of the galaxy, as best they can, as a sort of debris, or soot, that results from the perpetual fire of a plasma body, particularly a sun, that is beginning to exhaust its fuel and burn out, as it dies a heavenly death—referred to as a "supernova."

In this scenario, which is, in part, a correct analysis of cosmic mechanics, a star's mass becomes too weighty to sustain itself, and so it eventually implodes, resulting in a massive explosion—and then death, finality . . . nonexistence. But it is not death, as the astrophysicist intends it, that occurs in such triumphant moments of stellar exaltation. As we have now explained in several strategic points of our transmissions, the star is shedding the skin of its material form and accelerating into a higher dimension, where it will hold a new position, and resonate to a new vibration, in the Cosmos of Soul. That is a simplistic description of a very complex event, but then . . . all that we wonder about death, and what lies beyond physical life, are perennial, existential questions for every biological being, as they are for the stars.

As for interpenetrating layers of "interstellar dust," comprised of various gaseous forms, cosmic elements, rays, minute bits of carbon, magnesium, silicates, and iron, understand that this interstellar dust is not merely the soot and debris of a so-called "dying" star. It is, to the contrary, a very vital and conscious manifestation, one that permeates all space: within your star system, between stars, and across all the space in between.

No understanding of the solar system is complete if you consider it, like the models shown to you, as merely a central star and a smattering of planets and moons—with nothing but a void between them. What about the in-between: the interplanetary dynamics? What of the emanations of all bodies within the solar family, and their effect on the outer layer—the auric field of the sun? Know that about twenty percent of your sun's extended field is actually comprised of these tiny particles that play a crucial part in seeding life, across the great span of celestial bodies. They serve as delivery systems for intercommunication between the sun and the planets, and they carry the soul essence of beings, like you, who are starseeding the universe.

Organic or inorganic, all matter is a reflection of consciousness. If a door handle flies off a vessel and drifts off through space, it may not be described as biological matter, nor be considered to contain elements necessary for life, but you cannot deny that it certainly does express the consciousness and the intelligence that went into its creation. It speaks, to any eventual beholder, of the level of technical advancement of whomever designed it, of the resources available to those who crafted it, and of its possible function.

Therefore, we cannot discount inorganic substance. Even the smallest particle of dust or debris has a story. Under a microscope, it demonstrates how it, too, is alive. And we remind you, yet again, that all things are the creative and conscious interaction of protons, electrons, neutrons, and atoms. This is your own bodily composition, just as it is the substance of the multiverse.

This swath of very lively "dust," the interstellar medium, has an extraordinary function, which is important to your comprehension of the sun and planets, but more—to the evolution of galaxies. Most of the gas and dust particles contained within it are the product of stars in transformation, whether they are described as "exploding," or whether they are perceived as simply throwing off layers of their physical manifestations. Stars expel their substance into the realm of interstellar space, affecting the chemical dynamics of the galaxy, impacting interactive electromagnetic properties, ejecting organic compounds into their own space, and altering what lies between the stars.

Most importantly, however, is that within every speck of dust, within every molecule, atom, and grain formed by the stars and their emissions, there is consciousness. There is soul, traversing the heavens.

If you ask yourself, "How did I get here? Why did I choose to be birthed on this Earth, or in this star's system, so far from my home?" know that you are stardust, starseeding the universe.

From the flame to nested form, you are consciousness, determined, riding the solar wind.

14

Technology and the Mind Masters

Strip away the mind-numbing drone of discontent, fear, darkness, and violence that, like clay in the hands of a mad sculptor, is being impressed upon your psyches by manipulative forces outside of you, and you will be far more receptive to the natural state of grace to which life, in all its wonder, is born. Remove, or at the very least reduce, your fascination with the frenzied proliferation of technological gadgetry, your electronic control devices, and any and all other mechanical interference that entrains you, unwittingly, to frequencies that are not health enhancing for your mind, body, and spirit. You will experience immediate benefits: mental clarity, improved physical health, and the peace that comes from detachment from the control system—which is the network put in place to do just that: control you.

When you are racing to acquire the latest computers, games, phones, and other devices, always remember: the newer the technology, the greater is its debilitating effect upon you. It is designed, specifically, for that purpose. The more sophisticated its capabilities, the more invasive it is of your privacy and, as a natural consequence, the greater sway it has over your ability to think clearly and creatively, and to feel, from the heart.

Dare we say that when you are hypnotically glued to your device, removing yourself from everything else around you, you are blindly relinquishing your sovereignty? You may not want to hear that, for it is harsh—we do understand—and you may very well object to it—but we will speak it, nonetheless. The more entrained you are to it, the louder your objection will be to our bringing it into question. You may say that such a broad statement denies the positive aspects of electronic technology, and we do agree that, of course, there are positive applications. However, when we speak of the mind, consciousness, and the sovereign soul, the weight of what is being stripped from you far outweighs what you are gaining, as individuals, and as societies. If you think about it, objectively, and with true discernment, you cannot deny that it is so.

Moreover, the highly dangerous waves of electromagnetic radiation required to operate the system are coursing through your communities, your homes, and your physical bodies, causing unparalleled levels of cancers and other grave illnesses. This one fact, alone, should teach you that simply because something is invisible to you does not mean it is not there. It is operating on frequencies that are directly influencing yours, and interfering with all nearby biological beings (to include animals, plants, even the water lines) and other electronic equipment and devices.

We suggest that eliminating them, in the here and now, is a wonderful way to conserve your higher energies and to assist the planet. But of course, that is your decision to make.

In the following passage, we intend to elucidate how the overreach of technology is all part of the deliberate plan to reduce Earth's frequencies to the lowest denominator, by possessing all human consciousness within an electronic network of artificial intelligence, through which it can be redesigned, reconstructed, and eliminated, entirely, when it no longer serves the system. For that is the clear and present danger of the techno-maniacs—that is, to replace biology, in all forms, with robotics: mosquitoes, bees, and other life forms are already being usurped by robots. Are you aware? One might contemplate whether the annihilation of entire bee communities falls into the category of the deliberate elimination of one of your most vital species, for the sake of instilling a global, robotic swarm, self-replicating, that can be manipulated to perform their natural function.

This is the clear and present direction of the computer/technology industry, rapidly pushing human consciousness into artificial intelligence . . . and it is up to you—conscious beings—to reject it. It is up to you, the guardians of Gaia, to reverse the course that is taking you away from harmony, rushing to hand over your own humanity, and other species, to robot world.

We do understand the mesmerizing power of the entire global communication network, which appears to be such an incredible tool for you all, and it is not without its benefits—this we have never denied. However, the negative aspects outweigh the positive, and this is more recognizable to you when you understand that your entire planet is encased in probing satellites: some armed with weapons, aimed outwards, at space, and inwards, directly at primary targets upon the Earth; others, unarmed and seemingly less aggressive, are pivotal to the network that spies upon the human race and transmits directly into your minds.

Enhanced surveillance software, implanted in all electronic devices, is now public knowledge. Its designers and commissioners actually want you to know they have you in their radar; they love knowing that you are willingly acquiescing to their power. And yet, that still does not deter you. You do not rebel; you do not reject it. Proof of deleterious effects upon your overall health, from the electromagnetic radiation that emanates from electronic equipment, does not persuade you. And, because you do not deny it, but rather, bow to it, this net grows bigger and stronger around you, your homes, your cities, and even the entirety of your planet.

The fact that, despite all warnings and consumer information available, you still rush to acquire more, demonstrates how you have yet to understand the life-altering effect it has upon you. Or is it that you simply prefer to ignore it?

We are not so unrealistic to propose that it would be best for humanity if you were to completely banish the technological advancements of your twenty-first century. Our own transmitter, Trydjya, utilizes a computer device to bring our transmissions to form, in the written word. Therefore, please understand that we are not declaring technology, of itself, to be your only problem. What we are saying, and that which we have continued to impress upon you for over two decades of your time, is that we are highly concerned about technology's unrelenting grip over the nearly eight billion conscious minds that are directly or indirectly plugged in to the system—the global system—through which you are all becoming significantly entrained.

What is at question here is humankind's willingness to hand over its power in so many ways, primarily through this system, and that is what we intend to discuss in this missive. We do not stand in judgment. Our intention is focused and clear: we wish to help you all take back your power.

It always has been.

We believe there is a great urgency that you finally come to terms with the truth of how your electronic entrainment disempowers you: how it is dictating what you mentally ingest, and how you think, behave, and interact with it—as it rearranges your neural networks and reprograms your brain.

Moreover, it is a deliberate and well-planned deterrent to your creativity, to your perception of community consciousness, and to your unity with all living beings upon the Earth—and, eventually, from beyond.

You walk a tightrope between serving your own highest good, as individuals, and serving the communal good, neither of which is served by the electronics industry, which operates a very clear agenda: total enslavement of the population.

Yet, unlike slavery in its most obvious forms, this is far more insipid.

There are no physical chains here, binding you to servitude. It is your mind that is entrained, plugged in to an electromagnetic grid that is so mesmerizing it has you willingly serving the master.

You are running to it, eager for it, scrambling for every new model, every new design and added capability. In turn, it listens to you; it determines what you consume; it feeds on human consciousness and expands its grip over you.

Do you hear us, Children of the Earth Song?

It is feeding on you, altering you to respond to its needs, not the other way around, as you surely believe. That is simply not the case. You have passed the tipping point, where technology served you. Now, **you** are serving **it,** and this self-induced servitude, unrestrained, is about to fling you into an artificial reality that we know you do not desire, if you continue to succumb to its tantalizing mind games and maneuvers.

It does not want you to accelerate and raise your conscious vibration—it was designed to decelerate the progression of the collective consciousness. It does not want you to be sovereign of mind, body, and spirit. And now, as if it hasn't had enough, it intends to steal your biology from you, to reorganize your minds and all your cellular memory. It is preparing to completely rewire your brains.

You are already witness, as we foretold, to implantation of computer technology within the bodies of animals and humans alike. The push is on for all human beings to accept implantation before the end of this present decade: the technology industry, backed by global government, is actively pursuing it; the media is already pushing it upon you.

This is madness. Do not allow it.

If you can achieve enough objectivity to understand what lies ahead, in the far more dangerous technological advancements that will be rolled out to humanity in the next ten years, you will hopefully feel motivated to release yourselves from its hold. When you truly recognize that it is robbing you of your free will, and entraining you to that of the system (while, as a side effect, it is altering your mental, physical, and spiritual health), we believe you will be more willing to simply let it go.

You will almost instantly feel so much better, and you will be able to think with far greater clarity, as if an invisible fog has been lifted: a shroud that has been clouding your vision of a clear horizon up ahead, damping your hope that love will illuminate the hazy pathways of human evolution.

As much as possible, within the framework of utilizing what you deem "essential" from electronic technology, but limiting the mindless distraction that you embrace as "entertainment," you are going to need to redirect your consciousness. Your very future depends upon it. These are critical choices you are called to make at this time of imminent ascension.

Earth, your starship to the next dimension, is in the balance here. And the collective mind power of nearly eight billion consciousness units—the human flame—is at the crossroads.

We stand for the ideal that how you choose to interact with that disruption, on all levels, is strictly your decision to make. However, neither are we opposed to gently pushing you, lovingly and with no desired outcome, to recognize—or at the very least, to question—how you are entrained in a system that has, as its intention, the obliteration of creativity, of lofty pursuits, and of true human interaction in unity, where you stand together:

dialoguing, reasoning, and sharing your human experience. Remember: facing fear neutralizes it; evading what it is that stirs it within you entrains you to it!

As for the communications systems that require such proliferation of electromagnetism, bear in mind that their essential program is to monitor all exchange between you—every single thought and every word—while directing your thoughts and desires to a frenzy feed of the lowest denominators. You cannot deny that it has already had a devastating effect on the values and visions of your societies, even if you still are unable to conclusively monitor the devastating impact its harmful radiation emissions are having on your physical health.

Do not expect the governmental regulatory organizations to ever provide you with information that does not serve their interest, and that—of course—means the corporate aristocracy that pushes this system upon you.

Runaway technology, proliferating at an utterly insane pace on Earth, and from a place in space that can be defined as the planet's middle to outer atmosphere, is preparing the human race to embrace artificial intelligence to such a point that you will want to merge with it completely, to lose your humanity to robotics: a new species of biologically designed androids. It has all but convinced you that you can no longer reason, think, or communicate effectively without it. Unquestionably, it is teaching you to yield eloquence and poetic expression to abbreviations, shortcuts, and codes. You are learning its language, and forgetting your own. And it has persuaded you, and the children, that it is the superior form of amusement—across the board.

If you were born two decades or more ago, around the time we first began our communications, you will remember how much happier and healthier you were without it. Weren't you? From our own perspective, it was easier to reach Trydjya then, and for her to hold the frequency required for our exchange. As you can imagine, our transmissions are more effective when we are not disrupted by such invasive and pervasive electronic pollution, such as that which permeates your space.

Designed to perpetuate a dysfunctional global society, and to disempower individuals within a given society (particularly visionaries and intellectuals), these disruptive sources of disharmonious energies are internalized by you until their hypnotic power over you becomes so intensely overwhelming that you often lose your grip on the tightrope of your mind. You fall, precipitously, into a state of impotence, followed by hopelessness, succumbing to visions of a future that are everything that you do not want for you . . . and for the world.

This is a multileveled, emotionally evolutive process that consists of the following stages:

* Receptivity

* Passivity toward any and all interference with your sovereignty

* Acceptance of that interference

* Defensiveness of all devices, mechanisms, and programs as being "good for you and society"

* Defiance toward any alternative information, observation, or scrutiny that would interfere with your dependency or addiction

This may not apply to you personally, but, undoubtedly, you recognize it, at the very least, in people around you—particularly in the children, who have never known life without the ubiquitous "World Wide Web."

Viewing Earth from beyond the satellite crust that holds it in total surveillance from its inner atmosphere and extending to its outermost layer, the exosphere, we can tell you, without question or reservation, that this kind of "progress" is not the way of a peaceful civilization, and your galactic neighbors do not perceive you as one. This massive and almost impenetrable wall around the planet does not speak of a world that invites any life forms beyond its barriers to interplanetary or intergalactic exchange. In essence, it is a monumental "Hands off!" sign to all space travelers, except those who are aggressive and technologically advanced enough to disarm it, if necessary . . . or to simply ignore it and all that it represents.

It is designed to keep you in isolation, and that intention is built into and comes through your electronic devices. No matter who the perpetrators are, and no matter how diabolical their intent, your acquiescence is the greater problem; and so, we reiterate that you are wise to extract yourselves, as much as you possibly can—as soon as possible.

We recognize how these mechanisms are affecting so many starseed, who have come in with such suprasensitive awareness. The electromagnetic bombardment of your energy fields is utterly debilitating, but it is so subtle, it can be imperceptible at the conscious level. It is altering your subtle energy body, damping your spirit, altering your emotions, and eventually creating illness in your physical form.

All of these manifestations we consider disempowering to all human beings. We wish to see you filled with hope: empowered systems disrupters, living in the right now of your experience.

Won't you bring that strength and courage with you, when you transit the dimensions?

15

On a Crash Course with Artificial Intelligence

Your body is a perfect biocomputer, filled with the knowledge and informational codes of all Creation. Nothing can exceed its potential—no artificial intelligence can supplant it. Although you may believe computers and high technology can outprocess the human being, it is not true. Your biological being computes, so breathtakingly, the infinite data that determine the processes required just to move a finger that it would stagger your imagination if you ever gave it much thought. But, of course, you take it as a given . . . and rarely, if ever, contemplate the extraordinary intelligence and the spiritual nature of every cell of your body.

Yes, computers can process complex information that appears to be superior to your own innate mental capabilities, but that is due to the simple fact that you are still not operating all of your DNA light streams. Like an old-fashioned switchboard, several connections that rush information and stimuli through your neural networks are unplugged, and you are operating only a minute portion of your brain. You are being programmed to use even less, until such time as you have been made completely irrelevant by the takeover of artificial intelligence.

As we have described previously, most of the human race is operating on less than ten percent of its DNA information, holding your species in instinctive, animal behaviors of fear and survival consciousness. Unfortunately, for reasons that involve control mechanisms put in place by the ruling elite, as well as environmental factors diminishing the health of the organism, the additional ninety percent is relatively dormant . . . but it is still within you, receptive to impetus from your own mind.

It is coded into every human being, and it all serves a purpose: reconnecting you to your galactic knowledge and multidimensional wisdom. It is the gateway to simultaneous lives.

What they refer to as "grey matter" in the brain, and its corresponding disabled DNA (which they still refer to as "junk" within you), they have, nonetheless, been collecting from you, in DNA banks, and in covert experiments. This precious "junk" is being taken from you, in sweeping government and alien abduction programs that have been actively experimenting on you, for over half a century.

Its primary use by the secret government is to program artificial intelligence. For its partnering alien technicians, it is essential to the creation of hybrid races.

In these coming years, you will be witness to and participant in the awakening of the complex DNA matrix in vast numbers of human beings, rather than in only a select few who have achieved partial activation of those dormant threads, or who are born with more DNA illuminated. However, you must understand that how quickly you, as individuals and as societies, rise above the ego-centered, me/you, us/them consciousness will determine how rapidly the codes of knowing will realign, regroup, and rebundle within you.

You may not be the original creator of your biocomputer, but you were designed to be its programmer and, to a very large extent, to serve as its extended repair team—although its creator designed it to be self-repairing. You determine how efficiently it works to achieve states of greater awareness, peace, and understanding of the greater universe. You determine its health, efficiency, and balance, as much as possible, within the framework of a declining environment.

This electromagnetic, biological unit, which you know as "self," is capable of extraordinary computations, mostly occurring at the subconscious level. Just maintaining your body is such a monumental feat that you cannot imagine it: the millions of computations, instructions, and visualizations occurring simultaneously are utterly unfathomable to you, at the conscious level. But your DNA—the intelligent architect—knows exactly how to create what is necessary for the proper function of all aspects of being human, on Planet Earth.

The "junk" DNA, or rather, the ten complex strands of information that have been scattered within you, knows how to attune you to any place, any vibration, and any frequency in the multiverse. It holds all the keys to longevity, if you choose to remain in your present body; it holds the frequencies of other dimensions and parallel worlds, too.

You can understand why the ruling elite of Earth, intent upon owner-ship of the planet and subjugation of the population, do everything possi-ble to assure that you never regain access to that extraordinary information within you, waiting to be rekindled. If they can keep you in the duality of two strands of DNA, locked in, and rebuild human DNA for their robotic creations, then (they believe) they will have successfully destroyed human-ity, and replaced it with their monstrous creatures of artificial intelligence.

The AI designers, who have humanity careening toward a world of robotic machines, beings, insects, and programmed, synthetic flora, are today, more than ever before, actively programming you to see your world as a distorted, dystopian environment where the human being is no longer capable of creating beauty, harmony, and happiness. Their devices and cam-paigns against your sovereign will are intent upon entraining your minds to be alienated, rather than engaged, to hold tightly to a doctrine, rather than to give space to each other's beliefs, and to create your own suffer-ing—rather than nurturing peace and that "outdated" sentiment: happiness.

Some of you escape this manipulation; others drown in it. This has everything to do with how you use your minds, how you run your ener-gies, and, most importantly—how you use your intention to escape the jungle survival instinct, in your pursuit of higher consciousness.

If it were not enough that they are constructing hordes of robotic devices, they have made it very clear to you that you, too, are going to eventually succumb to being altered—and eventually lose your humanity to an implanted robotic mind. This future world is being imprinted on your consciousness constantly. You are surrounded by it. Always depict-ing their technological abominations as being for "the good of society," they have already begun implanting bionic body parts into eager human beings, and here come computer chips, being inserted, for the time being, just under the skin. From being chipped with a tracking device, to having yourselves implanted with information, like an exterior disk downloads data into your computer, you are being prepared to accept that your exqui-site minds are inferior to technology, and that it will be a requirement for life if you wish to be vital and effective in the new world—or rather, in the New World Order.

The question you need to ask yourself is this: once you are all chipped and controlled by technology, will you still require your biological forms? You already see people engaging with robots for comfort, conversation, and even sexual pleasure. When will you be made obsolete—and disposable?

The obvious direction of artificial intelligence will see your existence—mind, body, and soul—inserted into a robotic version of the former you. If that sounds eccentric, or overly paranoid, you are not paying attention to what is being created around you. Once your DNA is loaded into a robot, or implants are imbedded within you, and you accept artificial intelligence into your physical body—**you are the robot.**

The robotic models being thrust upon you seem so utterly dark and foreboding, but, actually, they are templates standing up to you as models of a possible future that you may or may not create. Some of you worship technology and cannot wait to integrate with the robotic techno-world, as if, on some level, you believe it to be the only way to achieve immortality. Others, seeking the realms of higher consciousness, observe the emergence of artificial intelligence with indifference, using their exquisite minds to choose the loving path that defines the potential that lies before every being, everywhere, in every state of existence.

However you perceive this rapidly advancing reality, know this: you do truly need to start making the right choices, right now. We, who observe you with love and concern, believe that this means unplugging, as much as you can, and disallowing anyone, or anything, to penetrate your divine space with technological devices, gadgets, and microchips.

That includes photosensitive tattoos—the new trend. They contain nanoparticles that you want as far from your skin as possible.

The decision of whether you will be your own, sovereign being, or a designer robot model of your former self, begins with the firm intention to eliminate technology, as best as you can, from your world.

And if you cannot resist, at the very least—keep it off your skin, and by no means allow it to enter the tissues and bloodstream.

The chip, the tattoo, the nanoparticles in the bloodstream, bionic body parts, the holographic brain implants . . .

This is not who you are, nor who you came to be.

16

Alien Outposts and
Extraterrestrial Inroads

We shall feel free to refer to any and all physical extraterrestrial life forms as "alien," bearing in mind that we mean no derogatory implication of that term, and impressing upon you that we are determined to represent the alien agenda to you with compassion, detachment, and unbiased consideration of its presence, and involvement, in your sphere. In fact, we prefer to speak in terms of the cause and effect of their activities, rather than to elaborate and describe what has already filtered into the collective unconscious, through a full spectrum of emotion-based depictions: from heinous creatures determined to destroy all humanity . . . to the glorification of angelic, Federation do-gooders, on a mission to save you all from the fate of a dying planet. We believe truth is almost always found at the fulcrum point, between the extremes, and that is what we wish to propose here, based on our perception of extraterrestrial interaction with human beings, and with select animal species.

While the lure of extraterrestrial disclosure, the proverbial "carrot," is perpetually being dangled in front of you, there are plenty of aliens already established on the Earth, mostly unnoticed by you. Aliens walk the halls of the Pentagon, interfacing with generals—and those to whom they, in turn, report—in the management of the alien agenda, and its interplay with covert military operations, across the board.

Dismissed as hoaxes, pictures of them interacting with several presidents, the military—even celebrities—have been shown to you . . . and that is a clever strategy, if you think about it. When the time comes that this truth is finally to be disclosed, a very few years away, your governmental agents and military brass can always say, "We showed you the pictures . . . you chose to deny them!"

You do realize that there is no better way to keep a secret than to put it right out there where you can see it, but not believe it? This is the way with aerial chemical spraying of every city and landscape, everywhere around the globe: that not-so-secret government operation that is turning your horizons grey and sunless, and poisoning the earth. And yet, people still deny that those gauze tongues of hazardous biochemical poison, smeared across your clear blue skies, exist in any way other than as a figment in the imaginations of deluded conspiracy theorists.

We leave it to you to consider what this says about collective distraction and human awareness, always celebrating those of you who are awake, and aware of what is going on around you.

In the realm of 3D illusion, something that exists, but does not conform to your idea of its nature, substance, or presence, can elude you—even if you are staring right at it! While you are waiting for disclosure—screaming for it . . . demanding it—the extraterrestrial reality is right in front of you, just as visible as those grids of chemicals overhead, and just as invisible . . . to those who refuse to see. The signs are ignored and dismissed by most, whose ideas of contact are far more cinematic than reality will ever provide.

By now, we have spoken so much of the Annunaki overlords that we feel you know them, or at least you know how we interpret their presence there and, certainly, their intentions. We do confirm that there are several other species involved in human affairs, in varying degrees, and with different agendas. Some are willing residents; others are imprisoned in military installations. There are approximately one hundred different races, beyond the Earth, currently communicating with "above top secret" operatives, and more who secretly observe your planet, concerned with military, technological, and ecological abuses, as they affect human and galactic evolution.

The stereotype that has taken seed in the human collective mindset, of extraterrestrials, is most frequently depicted through the classic image of the Grey alien, or Zeta Reticulan, with its huge black eyes, bulbous skull, and short, stocky body. Sometimes it appears as terrifying—sinister, and soulless; other times it is cartoon-like, even "fun." These human interpretations, which are based largely on expectation, subconscious implants, and pure fantasy, seem to somehow always misrepresent the reality of these beings—and their purpose for being so present in your realm.

Truthfully, Grey aliens are so devoid of emotion they are not capable of evil or goodness. They are sterile, almost robotic, technicians in the laboratories of hybrid experimentation, which, by the way, are no less foreboding than those human laboratories, where your own scientists perform similar experiments, or ones that are much worse, even torturous, on subjected animals.

Beyond that archetypal extraterrestrial character, there are truly countless species known to those of the "above top secret" agency that deals with alien intervention. Some of these are so human-like that they can be mistaken for humans—and often are. There are hybrids, too, with human DNA, walking around, undetected, in and out of government and corporate environments, and they do not appear to be any different from you.

But they are so different, energetically and, of course, genetically.

Those of you who read the energy body, as does Trydjya, can identify them—for their auric fields and vibrational patterns are not familiar energy grids. They are even more identifiable when you make eye contact, if you can penetrate their screens and look deep within those portals.

There are those that hover in space: the Watchers. Some are benevolent, others are not, and this, dear Gaians, is an absolute reflection of your own species.

As we venture deeper into the discussion of alien DNA, and the creation of new hybrid species, we find it opportune to remind you that you, too, *Homo sapiens,* are alien to Earth. You were nested there in the Great Experiment, from the collective seed of intelligent, compassionate beings beyond your planet, members of the Alliance for Intergalactic Commerce and Cultural Exchange. And now, in a small window of time, before the shift, you are on the threshold of migrating to other worlds—even to nearby solar systems, spreading your seed even further, out into the cosmic melting pot. And there are hybrids, moving about in space, that are part human. Mars, alone, is home to an alien/human hybrid civilization, taking hold there. Just remember that when you become frightened or uncomfortable with the idea that aliens are experimenting on select "victims," or abductees, for the sake of creating and propagating a hybrid race that will assure their survival.

When you think about that, it does put things into a different perspective, would you not agree?

To discuss the alien question, we need to jump back, just a moment, to the time of your Second World War, when Earth's pendulum swung so fiercely to the dark side, and two atomic bombs blasted open a new wave of alien preoccupation with Earth's warring potentialities.

Given our previous perspective on the term "alien," and, for the sake of fluidity of thought and its expression through the limitations of language, we will use it, intermittently, with reference to any other exoplanetary life form that is foreign to Planet Earth (Annunaki bloodlines notwithstanding) . . . or, shall we say, any exoplanetary life forms alien to the Earth, until a time that corresponds to the early twentieth century. At that crucial moment, highly trained Nazi occultists, determined to utilize advanced alien technology to conquer the entire world, pulled Grey Reticulans into Earth's realm telepathically. And they got very close to achieving that end . . . so close that the opposing team triggered the atomic bomb as a show of might and superior technology—the deterrent that effectively stopped the Nazi camp from achieving its objective.

Those powerful explosions, and the poisons they released, created quite a stir amongst alien nations, some of whom immigrated to Earth around that time. Theirs was a quest to understand what possibly could instigate human behavior to such an extreme that it would recklessly detonate atomic warfare: on its own planet, against its own civilization, and into its own delicate atmosphere.

It was not the devastation of the war itself that drove them to observe you, nor was it the archetypal villain who has been immortalized, in your history, as the greatest evil that ever walked the Earth. No, it was those atomic bombs, cast upon the innocent of the islands of Japan, which sent ripples through your atmosphere, into the body of the solar system . . . and across the waves of the Cosmos.

You are not supposed to remember that; historians have been successful in almost eliminating those two atomic bombs from human consciousness. You are almost all too young now to even remember. Certainly, the writers of history, and all politicians, want you to forget that the Alliance for "good" was the one—the only one—that deliberately, and with no regard for the consequence of its omnipotent act, unleashed atomic weapons against another nation.

Seventy years later: Fukushima. Those who observe you recognize the karmic significance in the fact that, from this nation, Japan, and its damaged nuclear power station, enough radioactivity has been released to create an extermination event of epic proportions, across the oceans and, eventually, all the land masses of the Earth.

None of your think tanks, scientific experts, military, or governments has made any great effort to contain it, as it spews radioactive material into the ocean—every minute of every day. Very few people are willing to consider that, much less to discuss it, and yet still they wonder why "good extraterrestrials" do not simply swoop down and clean it up for you: your mess, your responsibility, and your lesson to be learned.

Suffice to say that the human race is not advanced enough to know how to contain this force, and to this day, less than a century later, you are absolutely vulnerable to any manifestation of its highly volatile, devastating energy. In the hands of your military and despots, it is annihilation waiting to happen. And yet, you build more nuclear power stations and more bombs: bigger and more powerful than those that come before them.

Perhaps this gives you a clearer idea as to why alien ships hover over nuclear bases, where several of your top military officials have reported the mysterious disarmament of several nuclear warheads. There is an antidote to nuclear fission, but it is a dangerous and highly unstable process. However, capable extraterrestrial observers, and their trained engineers, are methodically disarming military silos of those countries with the greatest nuclear strike force, rendering the most omnipotent weapons in their arsenals inoperable.

Then, too, there is the emergence of the Nazi/ET underground base, at your southern pole, causing quite a stir—since it has been discovered, after so long a time lying buried under dense glacial ice—ice that is rapidly melting there. What more disclosure do you need, than the realization that these warriors of darkness were so involved with alien technology, to finally open the door to ET presence?

Pay attention to Antarctica. There is a prominent, active extraterrestrial base there, and several humanoid races that have merged with the German blood still operate in those extreme laboratories and military bases.

The controlled secret government media is doing its best to spin this discovery, but their own satellite systems have given you access to view every point of the Earth—even those covered over for "top security" reasons. The mere fact that they are so labeled tells you what you need to know. There is an emerging narrative that what is in the deep of Antarctica is actually Atlantis, and that there is a loving, benevolent race of aliens, the Arcturians (alternatively named Atlans, or Avians), there—and that they will emerge at any moment to bring light and positivity to the human race.

This is not truth, not as we perceive and understand it, and we do not concur with that hypothesis. There is no great light shining from below that pole, and what is there bears grave consideration.

Despite your doctored historical record, the creation and deployment of the atom bomb in your Second World War was not the first time in human history that humans harvested the atom as a force for destruction. You reached that level of self-destruction before, around the time of the fall of Atlantis, when nuclear force was unleashed upon the ancient lands of India.

There does exist a record of this event, the undeniable account of an atomic missile, or bomb, and its destruction of an entire civilization, in the ancient holy book of India. It reads:

> *A single projectile*
> *charged with all the power of the Universe.*
> *An incandescent column of smoke and flame*
> *as bright as the thousand suns*
> *rose in all its splendor . . .*

It was an unknown weapon:
an iron thunderbolt,
a gigantic messenger of death,
which reduced to ashes
the entire race of the Vrishnis and the Andhakas.

The corpses were so burned
as to be unrecognizable.
The hair and nails fell out;
pottery broke without apparent cause,
And the birds turned white.

After a few hours,
all foodstuffs were infected.
To escape from this fire
the soldiers threw themselves in streams
to wash themselves and their equipment.

—the Mahabharata

The immense power wrought upon your own planet, against your own species and on all life on the Japanese islands, in the fated year, 1945, was by far fiercer than what was unleashed in that ancient Indian war. Of great concern to your neighbors and beings from star systems beyond your solar gates is that, in the last seventy years, you have so accelerated your nuclear capability that you are now capable of causing immense destruction beyond the Earth—and like children playing with fire, your military governments seem more than determined to do just that.

This abuse of military might, and the immense ignorance of what ripple effect such weapons will have on the galactic environment, emerge when the governing body of any civilization possesses power that exceeds its conscious and spiritual development.

This is the trigger that renders the laws of noninterventionism inapplicable.

As we look to the present, we, and those who observe you from their physical positions in your greater galactic region, have determined that your combined military forces possess enough nuclear strike force to destroy Earth, and your moon, at least five hundred times over . . . to simply blow them both apart at the seams. Were they to be allowed to proceed, such an all-out nuclear war would create a cataclysmic event of such vast proportions that there is no way to even describe it—and we prefer not to send thoughts of such energies through our vibratory fields . . . nor yours. The potential of that much destructive power is beyond your scope completely, especially considering how little you understand space—the physical universe—and the higher dimensions.

What we can tell you is that, were they allowed to release thermonuclear Armageddon, Earth and your own moon would be blown to radioactive bits, projectiles careening through space, and out past your solar shield. Depending on their proximity, planets and their moons within the solar system would either be knocked out of orbit by the cataclysmic expulsion of earth debris, or be slowly irradiated and destroyed. The electromagnetic balance of planets, in relationship to each other, to their moons, and to the sun, would be irreparable: the solar system itself would dissipate and fall apart. Even the gentle fiber of interstellar dust would become far more radioactive, spreading their lack of compassion and their rage throughout space, destroying life far beyond your immediate world.

That is not going to happen. It simply will not be allowed.

The elite and their chosen few seriously think they can survive such a war—their war—by nesting underground, with their ten-year food and water supplies, and alternative energy sources . . . waiting for it all to somehow "dissipate." They have created entire cities there: movie theaters, swimming pools, and fully staffed medical centers. No expense is too great to the wealthy, who plan to wait out the devastation of a nuclear holocaust, should it occur, in comfort. It is always interesting to observe how the uninformed and unknowledgeable create their illusions, and how those who manipulate those gullible souls can extract even more power and wealth from them, by feeding their fears and fantasies.

Suffice to say that nothing could survive the thermonuclear war that you so fear they might unleash upon you: not on the surface, not in the substrata, and not in the center of the Earth.

But fear not, for they are not allowed to release this devastation—and the top puppeteers do know it. Despite all the saber rattling and the non-stop threats of total annihilation, they will be stopped. Although your military cabal seems uncontainable, with no apparent laws or governmental decrees to harness it—there is most definitely in place an extraterrestrial agenda to prevent nuclear war, beginning with (but not limited to) the disarmament of arsenals, above and below ground, and nuclear silos.

We reiterate, emphatically: once you reached the point where you became capable of destroying not only yourselves, but also the entire planet and beyond, all interplanetary rules of noninterventionism, and all restraints against extraterrestrial intervention, were lifted. So, if you wonder why you are hearing military leaks about strange happenings "of the third kind" at your nuclear warhead bases, and on seafaring naval vessels, that is the reason.

A warring, technologically advancing military tyranny, and a compliant Earth race, are of concern to the peaceful co-existence of planetary civilizations within your star system, and beyond—and hence, you will not be allowed to migrate from the planet until you are disarmed and awakened.

That may very well mean there will be wars in space. If that is what is needed to stop human/alien allied military activity beyond your borders, then trust that the Alliance is prepared to deal with that threat—and to bring it to an abrupt halt.

Returning to our initial discussion of alien residents established on Earth, the question of noninterventionism comes into play. Why were problematic extraterrestrials allowed entry into your sovereign space, if such laws applied? Your global government, represented by the president, Eisenhower, met with Grey aliens mid-century and negotiated a trade that was compliant with their demands, or as they prefer to think of them, their "terms," back at the time of that war. This "agreement" is in place to this day. It was a relatively simple exchange: unparalleled technology in exchange for access to the human reproductive system, via covert activity and secretive abductions of the innocent, in order to basically extract reproductive material that they would then use to yield a continuous harvest of Grey/human hybrids—a new species.

You may be surprised to learn that thousands of these hybrid children have already been sent off planet, testing the hybrid species' survival potential in other planetary environments. This means that human DNA, mutated with Grey genetic material, is being distributed across the material universe, so you can actually say that human beings have already migrated off the planet, if you consider a hybrid form of your biology definable as "human."

Theirs is not an evil design, although, of course, it sounds frightening to you. Rather, it is survival mind—calculated, cold, and unemotional. Species are perpetually interbreeding, creating new and stronger genetic lines; and, lest you forget, you possess incredible DNA. Do not forget that they are taking the "junk," too, which they are intent upon reweaving into highways of untold intelligence and physiology.

From what you have heard from the terrified accounts of thousands of traumatized abductees who have been subjected to their probes and surgical experiments—it surely feels evil, but do not confuse the survivalist need for human genetic material, with a necessarily sinister intention to cause suffering. The fact that alien experimentation is forced upon unwilling subjects, traumatizing most of them for life, is the part that most terrifies.

And then there is the reality that your own government sold out the human race.

If there is terror to be felt, surely it would be sourced in that betrayal.

Some alien operatives believe they can benefit from the escalation of destruction on your planet, but there are others there, serving to help mediate peace around the planet, and to help you progress, like other intelligent species that inhabit planets within your solar family, to a more evolved planetary civilization. As with all things in the polar field of opposing energies, there are also alien races that have your good at heart, and who are particularly concerned for the ecology of your planet. Never forget that, within the Earth, there lies the sacred world of Agharta, a settlement of light beings who appeared in the earliest hours of Atlantis—the pure, untainted world when that civilization was so young and so innocent. The Yzhnüni, whom we first introduced to you in *Atlantis Rising*, are incredible light beings who have been protected, within the Earth, for one hundred thousand years, and it is there that is found the true spiritual leadership of Gaia.

Known also as the "Atlán," this race of alien beings (if "alien" they still can be called) has dwelled peacefully, inside the planet, for as long as *Homo sapiens* has walked the surface. They will soon be merging with you, serving as the new leaders of Earth, moving into play when open contact with extraterrestrials of exoplanetary communities is established.

The most significant alien presence, in terms of the actual number of beings present, is found in several underwater bases, distributed around the globe. Hiding in deep waters, as well as entering and exiting from the middle of oceans in the night, is the safest shield from the all-seeing eyes of your military government. Of these structures, some are known to the Pentagon and its counterparts, and some are still unknown to them, impervious to their probes.

If you wonder why a global naval directive has military forces around the world bombing the oceans, and charting them with intense sonar and other electromagnetic pulses, be aware that it is not because, as they tell you, they are conducting "war games." Supposedly, these are designed to protect you from the ever-present threat of terrorists intent upon landing their nonexistent warships on your shores—ships that could never get within reach of you, considering the net of satellite tracking systems encasing the planet. Neither is it the risk that some hostile nation might be planning to slip a few submarines through the control nets of national waters, lurking in the deep . . . waiting, like hungry predators, to attack and conquer.

No, that paranoia scenario is subterfuge for such an immense, global assault on your oceans—a smokescreen. You surely see through it.

What is really going on, in your deep seas, is a deliberate and orchestrated sweep of the oceans designed to knock out any and all underwater alien bases that are not in compliance with the secret government—so secret that its directives against the oceans are issued from eight levels above presidential security clearance.

Pleas from the Great Whales and the Dolphin Beings, the Q'iquoq'i, have all been overridden. Despite token efforts, on the part of the military, and their unfulfilled promise to reduce the rape of the oceans, the bombs, microwaves, and excruciating sonar blasts continue, uninterrupted. Because of this, the Q'iquoq'i are slowly leaving you, proceeding to other dimensions or reincarnating, with their brethren, in more receptive planetary environments.

Of those alien colonies in the deep, several have been detected in the last ten years, and some have been annihilated, or are in various states of deterioration. Several have evacuated the Earth altogether. Those that remain have been successful, so far, in evading probes and military observation, by maintaining perpetual motion, like any sea creature that does not anchor to the seafloor. Their structures have been adapted to the underwater environment to such an extent that they have become almost impervious to the surveillance technologies currently available on Earth.

These are multiracial communities that are comprised of scientists, marine biologists, and actual aquatic beings who interact with your own. They are there to study Earth's vital oceans, not to destroy them, and they have no contact (other than evasive maneuvers) with your military. As such, they are perceived as menacing and a threat to the cabal, which wants to destroy them, just as they do with any remaining nation that refuses to comply with their mandates.

In the subsurface, and not to be confused with the inner world of Agharta, you have alien bases where, instead, there is a most definite interface with government, the military, and the corporate technology masters. These are inhabited by the Zeta Reticulans, and also taller Greys, who are directly involved, at the highest levels, with human representatives of "above top secret" security clearance. They are those who negotiated the terms in the exchange of technology for human genetics. They originate in the Orion constellation, where a clashing of forces, light and dark, is constantly holding the region in imbalance.

The different races buzzing around in your space, observing you, are many, particularly from nearby planets. More important than describing them to you, an exercise that we believe conveys low energy, and fills you with empty information, what we feel matters most is that you understand that you are surrounded by intelligent species: in the underground, in the sea, overhead, and walking with you, unobserved. It is not a future event to be disclosed; it is present, co-existing with you, in the right now of your experience. It is the announcement of this reality, and not the reality itself, that will be the new denominator, triggering integration with so many species, and revealing so many secrets that can be secret no more.

You are more than ready for this moment of reunion, eager for the days of isolation to end, and that is to say—whatever the outcome—you are ready for the film to be developed, for the negative image to be processed, in the light.

If we wish to expand the question of physical extraterrestrial beings and their interaction with you, and with your governments, it is because this is a reality that is going to be blown open, in the course of a very few years ahead of you, and it is absolutely, and without question, a key to your progression. In the greater scheme of reality unfolding there, it is no mere coincidence that this is happening now, at this turning point on your evolutionary wheel.

It is a catalyst that will unify most of your nearly eight billion people— exactly what those who have, for so long, held you in division do not want. A unified human race? That, we assure you, will be a force to be reckoned with.

From believing you are orphans in a lifeless universe, to encountering, en masse, dark and light extraterrestrial biological entities, you are going to be confronting and dealing with this explosive reality—which is going to show you the way to living with others, without hatred and rage—within a very few years of this transmission.

If you have been asking yourself "How in the world will we ever evolve from here to higher consciousness?" we assure you that learning how to accept alien species, and to embrace them, will by far exceed any challenge you have ever experienced in recent society. Finding the way to peacefully co-exist with beings that are both dark- and light-intended, and holding that balance, so that you can move forward in a paradigm that your grandparents could have never imagined, will be something quite extraordinary.

It will be difficult; it will be wonderful; it will be frightening and illuminating.

All this, in so many degrees, depends, as always, upon your intent, your perception, and your ability to embrace change—immense change.

It is best that you consider the wealth of information that is available with a sense of how this long-awaited encounter will affect the entirety. Ignore, as best you can, the cinematography that renders the pressing question of your future encounters with alien species an insurmountable terror, always bearing in mind that it is the "terror" of just about everything that has been used to facilitate the disempowerment of the human race.

What greater terror can there be, in your minds, than that of an alien race that has come to Earth to destroy all humanity, or to take over your world?

Always remember that if the intent of extraterrestrials—those already present, or studying you from afar—were to destroy you, you would already be gone, and your planet would be unrecognizable. That is a foregone conclusion. What they have given your military cabal in the way of weaponry and technology is just a sampler of the harnessed energies they have mastered and can use for destruction, if that ever becomes their resolve.

All of this will soon be relatively unimportant when the new wave of alien visitation arrives—that is, those beings who do honor sovereignty, and would never have intervened before the laws on noninterventionism were lifted.

That is the alien moment that you are all waiting for, and it will bring in forces of light who will help guide you through this quagmire of alien/ human interaction.

They will be loving, but resolute, in their intention to disrupt all existing alien/government treaties and agreements. They will be determined visionaries who will direct, but not command, you; and most importantly, they will be firm mediators between the powers that are falling away, and those new world leaders who will guide you forward.

You will know, without question, when they have arrived.

17

And So Goes the Reptilian Reign of Terror

Image by Anastasia Firsova/Shutterstock.com

We have abundantly elucidated, in previous manuscripts, how a very few power lords have successfully orchestrated a global control network over the entire planet, until now, when they are clearly losing their grip. We have described how they have operated their master plan over you, and over the Earth itself, exerting their power to significantly alter the course of human events over the millennia, while pursuing their primary objective for Nebiru.

Never, in all their time upon the Earth, have they been able to break the human spirit . . . although they certainly have tried, with all their cunning, their might, and their devices.

They, the Annunaki overlords, whose blood is unlike yours, are dying out now, and the empire is visibly crumbling. We did foretell of this time, and how you would come to realize it . . . and here it is. The kings, the queens, and those hidden dinosaurs of untold wealth and stealth, who have been sucking the life out of the Earth, from those gated kingdoms of the highest autocracy, have reached the extinction point of no return.

Their last generations, those who have been forced to accept what is, to them, the repugnant idea of breeding with humans in order to save their own species, have recognized that it is becoming more and more difficult to wear the disguise of human form. Their scales are showing through, and all is becoming transparent—far more transparent than any time before this, when they were capable of holding on to their secret, and ruling the Earth. But now, they are like vulnerable magicians, who can no longer tease your minds with illusions and trickery, created behind the drapes and veils of their self-ordained nobility—with all its gilded thrones, altars, and seats of immense power.

Those talons that have, for so long, held the human spirit in fear and obedience are disintegrating in the light of the new earth energies, releasing their grip over your entire world. It is more light than they can bear, light that—from their caves of darkness—is like staring into an eclipse, unprotected.

So, now, when you observe them "shape-shifting" from their human camouflage, to their reptilian skins, know that what you are seeing is actually their power weakening, and not what you may have believed was their strength intensifying. Remember that what is actually occurring is that, in the wake of such immense celestial energies bathing the Earth, and Gaia's own spirit rising, they can no longer successfully masquerade as humans, and that even life, in those reptilian underbellies, is becoming extremely uncomfortable on the blue-green planet.

If you are to rise above and erase them from your karmic memory, so that you leave them behind you, you do need to give yourselves permission to consider the cause and desired effect of their maneuverings against you, against the Earth, and—more recently—as a menace to any outside force determined to assist you in the battle they have waged against your planet. It is so important to understand that, and to observe them with objectivity, from one pole to the other, so that you are allowing your exquisite mind to see . . . to consider . . . and to experience the broad spectrum of possible realities. This is going to be tantamount to your achievement, and ease with the enhanced awareness that comes from your interfacing, and eventual transmutation into the fourth dimension.

From this blip in time, a mere twenty years since our first messages to you, to this moment, there has been a huge shift in the Annunaki primary directive that regards their desperate attempts to save their ancient home base, Nebiru, from galactic death.

These reptilian overlords of Earth, and their hybrid brood, have failed. They have realized defeat, although they still have not accepted it, and now seek solutions to their own survival. No amount of electromagnetic manipulation, nor any attempt to alter the space-time continuum to pull their planet, Nebiru, out of deep space, into your system, has succeeded. This, they finally conceded at the closure of the year 2012, when they saw the Wheel of Ages turn.

Despite what you hear of this "Planet X" arriving into your solar system, and all the disinformation being disseminated about that celestial body, we emphatically state that Nebiru is not within your solar system. It remains well outside of it, in galactic night, far from your star: too distant, that is, to achieve the far-reaching goal of attunement, or electromagnetic twinning, with your own planet—for the sake of a free ride into the fourth dimension.

They know now that their wandering planet, and its dying civilization, can never reach resonance with yours, no matter how much they have attempted to reduce Earth's vibratory essence. Gaia is strong. She is brighter and more luminous, at the very core of her being—her soul essence.

Granted, Gaia is struggling with several invasive factors that are attacking her immune systems, her regenerative capabilities, and her harmonic resonance, and she is rebelling with every ounce of strength she possesses. You are witness to her raging storms, decaying outer crust, and all manner of violent weather patterns. Some of these are the explosive energies of her rebellion against those injustices being perpetrated against her; others are deliberate manipulations of the secret government, which still insists on destroying the spirit of your planet, for as long as they can strip the planet of its wealth, essentially turning it into a mined fueling station for extraterrestrial merchants of future space wars now being instigated in your sector of the galaxy.

If you believe that the daily eco-disasters occurring around the Earth are "accidents," then you have not fully understood the strategic, systemic destruction under way—and we hold to the belief that it is of the utmost importance that you do. Gaia is under attack by sea, through atmospheric poisoning, and the dismembering of her skeletal essence—the earth. The epic disaster that you know as the *Deepwater Horizon* oil spill, in the oceanic region of the Gulf of Mexico, was no accident. This petroleum-rich body of water has been claimed by the oil lords, who are systematically emptying it of all its natural reserves. What comes of that process is a cultivated algae-biofuel plantation for future harvesting. This is not unlike the annihilation of huge swaths of rain forests, the lungs of Gaia, replaced by gold mining in parts, farming of animals for human consumption in others, or plantations of nonindigenous trees for the manufacture of high profit, low quality foodstuffs.

They are mining your DNA, and mining the resources of the Earth.

No matter how tightly these individuals wish to hold the reins of the human collective, you are entering a phase of galactic co-existence: from the 3D perspective, and from the future four-dimensional position. Remember: the laws on noninterventionism have been lifted. Beings from outside the quarantine that has held Earth in isolation for the last millennium are already interfacing with you, as a civilization and as individuals, even if it still does not appear that way, nor conform to your idea of how and when it will be clear to your entire population.

The reign of reptilian terror is almost up, and they know it. Their New World Order will not take hold—you simply will not let it, and you have enhanced energies that assure that it will not. It is a failed experiment, dying its first stages of death, and they have nothing left to replace it— nothing but the imposition of a one world, tyrannical religious authority, into which you are being indoctrinated, around the world. However, not even this menace will dissuade you, for you see through them now and, by seeing, you are undoing the knots they wish to tie around you. Against every possible power structure, against untold surveillance, police state governance, poisoning, and mind control, you still are breaking loose.

Their struggle, believe it or not, is far greater than yours.

Always remember—they are two thousand; you are almost eight billion. Holding that many human beings in division, rage, and fear has required a monumental ability to control your minds, and to perpetually instigate your emotional instability. It has been very effective until now. In fact, it has reached a pinnacle since you moved into the next galactic cycle, where everything is accelerating.

Even darkness is in a frenzy, turning against itself! This happens when the mighty cogs of evolution turn, and the rust-encrusted wheels must be liberated, so that they can spin freely. It clings, magnetized to the past, unwilling to let go, despite the disintegration of their dreams and the misguided power that generated them.

That is not to say that they no longer control the system: they do. But the system itself is dying—it is a crumbling empire, yielding to a revolution of human awareness.

They have pulled out all the stops in this final grip over the Earth, determined to bring you down with them, but your numbers now—and your understanding of consciousness over matter—are too insurmountable for their plan to be effective. It is not going to happen, and so you see them scrambling, manically, to save themselves. They have built infrastructures on the moon and upon Mars so that survival there is not only a possibility—it is already a reality. Their migrations have already begun. But what happens to them, when both of these planetary bodies ascend to the fourth density, is going to be determined by the intensity of the karma they bring with them.

It will not be easy; of this we are certain. With what we know of cause and effect, we have great empathy for the karmic debris that will pervade within and around them, until they are capable of resolving it.

As evil as they have been depicted to be across the ages, we remind you that these dark souls have had one primary objective behind their tyranny over the Earth—that is, to save their own planet, and the dying reptilian civilization—an entire species—that has barely managed to survive in its marauding, subterranean world. It was their hope to serve as saviors to an entire world—and although their idea to lower the Earth's vibration to resonate with theirs was utterly disruptive to your planet, it was the only hope they held for theirs. That remote and unreachable goodness, buried in their misdeeds and invasive presumptions over earth sovereignty, empowered them in many ways.

We are not asking you to find forgiveness for all that they have inseminated on your world, but we wish—for your own sake—that you can feel compassion. It is our hope that you are able to release the anger, the disdain, and your fear of them, to watch all those lower emotions dissipate in the light of the golden age upon you.

Your compassion means nothing to them. They do not seek your compassion—only your obedience, and so it does not matter to them at all whether you feel it or not.

But it will matter . . . to you.

And that is so precious, and so important.

18

The End of the Old-Ways Days

Despite the mechanizations of war and destruction that currently plague your planet, despite the seemingly insurmountable division being stimulated amongst you, we can tell you that the "end of the world," as it is being described to you, is a false projection of reality, designed to disempower you, flat out—until you have no way back to the heart center of your true humanity.

Many ancient prophecies were interpreted as doomsday scenarios of apocalyptic proportions, and there is no question that you are witnessing, on a massive scale, a growing fear-based conviction that you are, indeed, at the doorstep of the dreaded biblical "End of Days."

Back when most of you were asleep, you were numb to the fear. Now, as you reach the critical juncture, you see more people becoming more and more enraged, and, hence, this core fear of survival is now manifesting as violence, pitting one against the other, religion against religion . . . and nation against nation.

That perpetual, infinite threat of annihilation, and the stimulation of your lower energy vortices, allows those who wish to control you a more or less guaranteed and predictable behavior that can be directed according to their specific intention. In their last desperate push to hold on to control, the power that has ruled for so long has stimulated society, across the world, to new levels of hatred and rage. Race, gender, religion, age, money—all of these are the tools used to turn human beings against each other. And it has been marketed and implemented very successfully, across the ages—but never so much as now.

This is indeed the hour of your liberation, and the rulers of the old ways know, but they don't even know how to let go.

There is no record of true social freedom in your collective consciousness—there is only the illusion of it, and you are rewriting that paradigm with the light of your soul, climbing higher.

Weighed down in the lower energy centers that comprise your electromagnetic, biological makeup, human beings are being constantly manipulated to discredit any other belief system that does not conform, including violence and even indiscriminately killing those who dare oppose the masters. At this level of disharmony, one can easily perceive every word, action, and idea that lies outside of the comfort zone as threatening, menacing, or evil. So overwhelmed by constant, perpetual bombardment of the lower energy centers, it is easy for you to understand how trust in love and the pursuit of true happiness can seem to be diminished to nothing more than the impossible dream.

And soldiers, who fight for an ideal, believe it is the real purpose of war. They are willing to give their lives for it.

But you know better.

Do not lose your faith in humanity. The antiquated model of civilization in perpetual struggle will soon be replaced with a new fraternity.

On the surface, it may very well appear that the End of Days is upon you, for the levels of disharmony unquestionably challenge the idea that light is the pervading force in your world. But, if you look deeper, if you really dig down to the very core of your social and planetary instability, you cannot help but recognize that Earth is in the throes of enormous change . . . much needed change . . . and that, from it, something new and exciting is evolving.

The Great Wheel of Ages is turning—and it is on new beginnings, and not the tragic End of Days, that you are learning to focus your vision of human evolution. The old ways cannot resist the strength and the sheer splendor of the new, and they must yield, or self-destruct in the energies that are coming in now—energies that are guiding the course of civilization, providing each of you with new tools with which to re-create your lives.

One of these, perhaps the most significant of all, will be that open contact—undeniable, global exchange with alien races—will catapult your civilization to extraordinary new heights. We are telling you that within your lifetime, humankind will be interfacing with beings from neighboring planets, and from other star systems—and that it will be a positive exchange. You will be witness to humanity's reach beyond its limitations, dispelling your fears and despair, and guiding you to step courageously past the borders and walls of your mental, emotional, and physical containment. Then, soon after, you will take that cosmic ride through your sun's astral cord, into the next dimension.

To say that you have so much to look forward to is an understatement of unparalleled proportions!

Bear in mind that the disclosure process is not going to be what society is being programmed to envision: the menace of alien ships hovering over your major cities, or troops of space visitors marching on your capitals. That is a setup; it is the terror model, and you know that those who hold the controls love keeping you in terror while they instill within you the illusion that they (and only they) can protect you from it.

How many social and personal freedoms have you handed over, in the name of that "safety"?

Know that the last terror card in the deck is the one that depicts aliens invading the Earth. Be aware. The sky is your new viewing screen. It is already being utilized to project holographic visions into your psyches, and to confuse you as to what truth there is in the UFO/ET scenario, when that drama finally unfolds.

So many individuals want to own this information, and that includes some of your own alternative speakers and "researchers." So, turn up your discernment meters and filter the obvious from the sublime, for this is not going to be a box office production. If you are really paying attention, you will recognize how the obvious, the stereotypical, and the most iconic portrayals, beamed across the skies, will be as apparent to you as gross plastic fibers would be in a finely woven tapestry. Look for the fine silk threads, and the lace, to see where the real picture is emerging.

You have so many wondrous things to build now, a whole new way of being human. So much will surface within so very few years, and it is the turnaround point for your society at large, just as it is a part of the incredible energy that catapults you through the cords of the rising sun.

The end of the old ways is being revealed. The new is breaking, right now, on the horizon, and to some it looks frightening, chaotic, and irresolute, while others can see the light of brilliant days ahead.

Where have you placed your focus?

We have shown you how your progression into the fourth dimension has begun to manifest—you are at the outer limits, for lack of a more comprehensive term to describe the interface between dimensions. There, where you currently sit, you still appear to be very much glued to the third dimension, and yet there is a growing awareness that something is dramatically different everywhere about you. You are at the edge, bridging the third and fourth dimensions, moving through this difficult, but exciting, transition. You are beginning to experience the slipping of the space-time continuum, coming into contact, consciously, with alternative universes or realities as they filter in and out of your growing awareness.

A highly determined and organized network, which has, as its intent, the desire to keep you glued to the lower frequencies, is opening portals on the lower astral, and this is leaking entities that are not at all desirous, into your reality. From the light realms, beings of immense light and beauty are pouring in through gateways that lead into your solar system, through the immense portal that lies within the multidimensional star system of Sirius—the gateway of your galaxy.

With so much taking place around you, you are bound to feel unsettled at times, and we invite you to know it—to explore it—and to realize that there is a vast difference between security and balance. The first locks you into a way of being that does not want change to upset the status quo; the second finds the equilibrium to move with change, with grace, and with the fearlessness that comes from inner strength and unbridled love for all things . . . and all beings.

To all of you—lightworkers, starseed, brilliant souls—we sound the call. Let your emotions be calmed in still waters, and your minds be filled with the light of hope, empowered. Set your sails toward the horizon. The Earth is turning. Despite the devices of the misguided, and the fears of lost and distracted souls, remember that all is in divine order: it always has been; it always is; it always will be.

Our love surrounds you.

We are the Speakers of the Sirian High Council, closing communications in this significant calendar day of 4/22 in the year 2017. We leave you, in gratitude to the transmitter, Trydjya of Antares, and in celebration of the great human spirit with which we will have made contact, through these written words, and through the energies conveyed from the sixth dimension, to your world, in transition.

EPILOGUE

2017—the present. We are awakening in huge numbers now, and even the most determined sleepwalkers concur that something immense is happening on Planet Earth. Some see it as the hour of the apocalypse, some see it as the time of ascension—but what matters is that most of us recognize the end of a cycle . . . one that we happily wave away.

Let the new one take us to higher ground: a place of peace and celebration.

We conspiracy theorists have been exonerated—the proverbial cat is out of the bag. Everywhere, people are being emotionally blasted by the consequences of human obedience to a system that, as the Council say, is crumbling all around us. Through the confusion, fear, and rage, we are somehow dealing with it—but we are ready for change. We long for it.

We are the ones who must lift the chains from our necks, and only we can remove the shackles that we have willingly placed around our feet, deterring us from walking our truth.

The secrets that have bound us to our own ignorance of what really determines events on our planet are secret no more.

Donald Trump has been elected the forty-fifth president of the United States, and he is struggling, at the time of this writing, to stay in the presidential power seat. Benjamin Netanyahu still holds the position of prime minister of Israel, the most powerful position in that country's political arena. Prince Charles has taken his second wife, Camilla, hoping to take the throne as well.

And the planet spins, and the old yields to the new.

Despite the orchestrated animosities between NATO and Russia, down here on the surface of the Earth, a Russian cosmonaut, Fyodor Yurchikhin, is commanding Expedition 52, part of a program of crew rotations for the International Space Station, in alliance between NASA and its international partners. Apparently we seem to get along better in space than we do on the Earth—or is the perpetual "cold war" just a ruse to keep us on the edge of our seats, fearing Armageddon?

Although exact figures for 2017 are not yet available at the time of this writing, it is estimated that the total U.S. federal debt reached $20 trillion in the first quarter of this year, and it is estimated to burgeon by another trillion within the decade.

There are 7.5 billion people on the planet, and, if growth rates continue as they are, we will top 8 billion within a few years.

Iraq, Libya, and Syria are destroyed: their infrastructures have been leveled; the soul of the people has been shattered; the post–poisonous war environments have been rendered highly toxic and will remain polluted indefinitely. Their rulers have been neutralized or slain (or are living in style somewhere in a luxury compound in South America). The dead are buried, the desperate continue to die in vain or to flee to countries around the world, seeking asylum—and that, in turn, is sparking the new global crisis of unmanageable immigration that is socially, economically, and eco-logically disruptive on almost every level.

All of this suffering and destruction was utterly unnecessary, and so vilely inhumane, but so profitable for the perpetrators. The special few of the "aristocracy" that still positions its soldiers on the Risk[13] board of real life have become richer than even they could imagine. And the world, our world, has become a much poorer place: where our humanity, and the standards we deem essential for a "happy" life, are diminishing, across the board.

Television has yielded to the computer; the computer has given way to the smartphone; the phone is being replaced by digital implants—and just ahead, within their reach, lies the ultimate goal. Human DNA, and all of our intelligence and emotion, is being genetically and artificially merged to create an entirely new species: robotic cyborgs. All of this, in the name of "progress," of course, is being driven and consumed by human beings who,

---

13   A board game invented in 1957: https://en.wikipedia.org/wiki/Risk_(game)

consciously or unconsciously, are willingly handing over their sovereignty to artificial intelligence.

It is as much a travesty to behold as it is a difficult challenge to overcome. But we will.

Wherever this incredible Shift of Ages is headed, to whatever dimension fate and our karmic imprint propel us, it is our divine destiny to deliver Gaia—in her grace, and in all her glorious colors, scents, and song—through the clearing station of the fourth dimension and beyond, wherever that may take her.

We came here to do that.

So, let us think clearly; let us walk in the light of Spirit, and never be blinded by the hypnotic lull of an automaton world. A world where all is robotic and soulless is just unthinkable; it is against our humanity and against Gaia herself.

Oh, and lest we forget . . .

The powers that be would have you believing that we are about to migrate off a scorched Planet Earth and set up shop on Mars. It's a manifest destiny kind of thing, playing out again in a bigger hemisphere.

That Bill Clinton Martian rock served its purpose.

Anyone paying attention to the wealth of information surrounding Mars—information that has been leaked, or discovered by the new astronomers—knows that there is more life on Mars than ancient bacteria. Structures, statues, transport systems appear everywhere in the official images, and even those tampered with speak to us of truth that can no longer be hidden. If we are seeing them, it is because they want us to see them. They want us to believe that we are emigrating off our own planet, as the next step to human/robotic evolution.

The terraforming of that planet is successful—poles are melting, ancient forests are emerging, and surface life is rebounding, which has everything to do with the studied and soon to be executed plan to send the first wave of new settlers to join the underground Martian and human technicians there, in the rebuilding of a civilization: one that will be fraught with hybrids, robots, and chimeras.

Let's be real, here. We know NASA is all over Mars—how many rovers now? What other countries are rovering about in the new domain, preparing for the invasion of a reptilian-ruled human society that has still not progressed, in the words of Michio Kaku, from "a level zero society, where we burn our own fossil fuels, to a level one society, where we have learned to harness the sun's energy for all our energy needs"[14]?

None of these mechanizations matter now. We don't get to escape the mess we've made on one planet, only to invade another, without facing serious karmic repercussions. That just does not fit with anything we understand about cause and effect, and the karma of our own creations.

No, we will sooner experience Mars in the fourth dimension than to see it colonized by huge numbers of human immigrants. It too will be cleansed of any karmic baggage, and then propelled into its station—in a parallel universe perhaps, or in another dimension—after it clears the fourth density.

Who knows?

If the Sirian High Council is right again, we will soon be past all the dark maneuvering, well before the human race has been obliterated by a soulless robot civilization, commandeered by manic technicians who have lost their souls on the assembly lines of their own creations.

And remember, when you are feeling afraid, or hopeless . . . or when you long to return to your star, wherever that may be in the heavens, always remember:

They haven't been wrong yet.

[14] Patricia Cori, *Beyond the Matrix.*

ABOUT THE CHANNEL

 A native of the San Francisco Bay Area, Patricia Cori is a world-renowned author, public speaker, and activist for the rights of human beings and animals, a warrior for Planet Earth. A proven sensitive, she has been exploring mysticism, philosophy, ancient civilizations, metaphysical healing, spirituality, and unexplained mysteries and teaches on these subjects to enthralled audiences around the world.

She is considered a luminary of these times, and her work is embraced for its dedication to challenging the status quo and opening new vistas on human awareness.

She is a prominent figure in the Spirit Community, well-known on the international lecture circuit—actively offering courses, seminars, and workshops on a vast range of topics, which reflect her broad knowledge of alternative methodology in healing and her remarkable gift of helping others rekindle and ignite the flame of power within us all.

Cori has been recognized and celebrated as a gifted shaman by indigenous spirit teachers of the Tibetan, Mayan, and Peruvian traditions and has been embraced by the shamans of Palenque as one of the four spirit guardians of that sacred site. In 1996, she established the LightWorks travel club, SoulQuest™ Journeys, and that year led a group of spirit travelers to Nepal and Tibet. She has since guided people through sacred sites in Asia, Mexico, Egypt, Europe, Peru, the crop circles in England, and dolphin swims in the Azores, to contemplate the potential of interspecies interaction and our heightened sensitivity to the world that surrounds us. In every case, she has opened the portals and helped people experience the other side of the veil.

Her books, the trilogy The Sirian Revelations (published by North Atlantic Books) and an impressive collection of additional works across the years, have enjoyed worldwide acclaim as wake-up call material for the expanding consciousness of humankind, tools for empowerment and guidance. They are considered "must-have" reading for a global audience of seekers.

To learn more about her courses, workshops, and speaking engagements, go to www.patriciacori.com.

ALSO BY PATRICIA CORI

available from North Atlantic Books

The Emissary
978-1-58394-706-7

Beyond the Matrix
978-1-55643-893-6

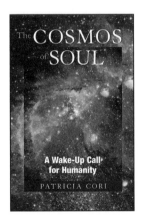

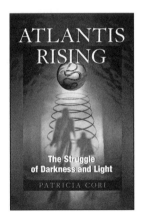

The Cosmos of Soul
978-1-55643-736-6

*No More Secrets,
No More Lies*
978-1-55643-738-0

Atlantis Rising
978-1-55643-737-3

North Atlantic Books
www.northatlanticbooks.com

North Atlantic Books is an independent, nonprofit publisher committed to a bold exploration of the relationships between mind, body, spirit, and nature.

About North Atlantic Books

North Atlantic Books (NAB) is an independent, nonprofit publisher committed to a bold exploration of the relationships between mind, body, spirit, and nature. Founded in 1974, NAB aims to nurture a holistic view of the arts, sciences, humanities, and healing. To make a donation or to learn more about our books, authors, events, and newsletter, please visit www.northatlanticbooks.com.

North Atlantic Books is the publishing arm of the Society for the Study of Native Arts and Sciences, a 501(c)(3) nonprofit educational organization that promotes cross-cultural perspectives linking scientific, social, and artistic fields. To learn how you can support us, please visit our website.